A WORD
TO WOMEN

BY MRS. HUMPHRY
("MADGE" OF "TRUTH")

AUTHOR OF
"MANNERS FOR WOMEN," "MANNERS
FOR MEN," ETC.

London
JAMES BOWDEN
10, HENRIETTA STREET,
COVENT GARDEN, W.C.
1898

PRYOR PUBLICATIONS
WHITSTABLE AND WALSALL

MEMBER OF
INDEPENDENT PUBLISHERS GUILD

A WORD TO WOMEN

FIRST EDITION . . . . . *April,* 1898.
SECOND EDITION . . . . . *May,* 1898.

© 1996 Pryor Publications

75 Dargate Road, Yorkletts, Whitstable,
Kent CT5 3AE, England.

Tel. & Fax: (01227) 274655

Specialist in Facsimile Reproductions.

ISBN 0 946014 52 3

A CIP Record for this book is available from the British Library.

Printed and bound by
Biddles Ltd.

Woodbridge Park Estate,
Woodbridge Road,
Guildford GU1 1DA

PREFACE

MY book " Manners for Women " has met with such a kindly reception that I am encouraged to follow it up with the present little volume. Of a less practical character than the former, it yet follows out the same line of thought, and is the fruit of many years' observation of my countrywomen in that home life for which England is distinguished among nations.

C. E. HUMPHRY.

London, 1898.

CONTENTS.

CONTENTS.

8

A WORD TO WOMEN.

—◆◇◆—

MOTHER AND DAUGHTER.

THERE is a happy medium between narrowness and latitude ; between the exiguity which confines the mind between canal - like borders and the broad, expansive amplitude which allows it to flow with the freedom of a great river, though within certain definite limits. The tendency of the moment is towards breadth and the enlarging of borders, the setting back of frontier lines, and even to ignoring them. " One must move with the times " is a phrase constantly heard and read. It is true enough. One would not willingly be left stranded on the shores of the past; but then, in the effort to avoid this, one need not shape a wild and devious course. There is always the golden mean attainable, though occasionally it needs some seeking to find it.

The golden mean.

In nothing so much as the relations

between mother and daughter is this modern tendency prolific of

Some modern daughters. difficulty. For some generations the rule of severity that began with the Puritans has been gradually relaxing more and more, and now the spectacle of a harsh-voiced, domineering young woman, ordering her mother about, is by no means an infrequent one, detestable as it is. Nor does she always content herself by merely ordering. Sometimes she scolds as well! If the mother, in these revolutionary times, has any chance of maintaining her own position as the elder and the wiser of the two, she must keep her eyes open to the successive grooves of change down which the world is spinning. The daughter must not be permitted to suspect her of old-fashioned notions. That would be fatal!

When the bicycle craze began many mothers disapproved of the exercise for their girls. But with

The bicycling craze. doctors recommending it, and the girls themselves looking radiantly bright and healthy after a few preliminary trials, what remained for the mother but to overcome her first dislike and do all she could to persuade the father to buy bicycles for all the girls? The next step was, often, to learn to ride herself, and to benefit enormously thereby. The mother who failed to follow her daughters' lead in this particular, as in

others, proved that she was too narrow
to accept new ideas; just the sort of
thing to give the daughters a lead in
these century-end days. And of that
one must beware! The poor mothers
must not give a single inch, or they
will find themselves mulcted in many
an ell.

The old, strait-laced ideas about
chaperons are now decidedly behind
the times, and the parents and
guardians who try to maintain
them in all their rigid inte-
grity will only find that the
too-tightly-drawn bow will
soon snap. Far better to accept changes
as they come, taking the wide, enlarged
view, and allowing the young creatures
as much freedom of action as may
be consistent with the social laws.
The old parallel of the hen-mother and
the young ducks would come in most
usefully here, were it not so hackneyed.
But think what sad deprivations of the
joie de vivre the ducks would have
suffered had it been in the power of
the hen to enforce her objections.
Think of this, oh ye nineteenth century mothers! What trepidations,
what anxieties, what feverish fears,
assail us when the young ones escape
from the restrictions that bound ourselves when we were girls! The father
laughs at our tremors, and proves, by
doing so, what needs no proof, that
the sense of responsibility is always
deeper and keener in the mother, and

About Chaperons and Chaperon-age.

that, therefore, she is more bound than he to exercise due caution. To combine the two with wide views is not always easy.

"These affectionate women," said Sir Andrew Clarke, the eminent physician, "they make themselves **"The evils that never arrive."** miserable about things that may happen, and wear themselves out in anxieties for which there is little or no foundation." And Jefferson says : " How much have cost us the evils that never happened !" True, indeed. But, also, how much have they cost to the objects of our care? Can any one reckon up that difficult sum? The timid, fearful mother has often ruined her boys out of pure anxiety to do her very (mistaken) best for them. And as to girls, they are not allowed to do the very things that would teach them self-reliance, make them vigorous in mind and body, and teach them that lore, not in any girls' school curriculum, which is best expressed in the French idiom, " *savoir faire.*"

And all for want of width ! What sort of life would a little chicken lead **Want of width.** if it were for ever under the good old hen's wing ? Yet that is what some of us would prefer for the bright young things, whose very life is in change, variety, excitement, fun, laughter, and exercise of all kinds. Small wonder that some of them rebel, feeling tethered, with the inevitable longing for escape. Led with a silken string in wide ways of the great world, they would be contented and happy enough.

Every girl is a queen to some one at some time in her life. Was there ever a girl whom nobody loved? What would English homes be without their girls? Mothers of sons are proud indeed, but they often long for a daughter.

Mothers and daughters. The tie between girl and mother is a wonderfully close one. They almost share each others' thoughts, and the home life together becomes, as the girl grows up, a delicious duet. Sons, however affectionate and gentle, have always some part of their nature veiled away. They cannot tell all to a mother as a daughter can, with perfect open-mindedness, so that the page lies clear to the eye of affection, like a book in good, large print. And more particularly is this the case with an only daughter. Have you ever, dear reader, noticed how the tendrils of the growing vines twine round each other, at last becoming so inextricably close that they cannot be separated without breaking them? That is the way that many a mother and daughter whose lives are closely woven in with each other, forming a bond of strength that, with the flowing of the years, increases in power and influence.

And then comes some charming young

13

man, with pretty eyes and a gentle manner, and oh! the loneliness of the poor mother when he carries off her girl to be the sunshine of his home, leaving hers in deepest shadow!

The inevitable man.

But mothers are unselfish and love to know their daughters happy, fulfilling their destiny in the good old womanly way as wife and mother. And the best way to make a girl a good wife is to train her to be a first-rate daughter.

A girl's thoughts of usefulness sometimes begin a very long way off. They appear to her at a distance, as if she were looking through the small end of a telescope. "The thoughts of youth are long, long thoughts," and the girl's idea of usefulness is to nurse the sick and wounded in war-time, to go out as a missionary among the heathen, to write books with great thoughts in them, to do noble deeds of tremendous self-sacrifice, to take up some great life-work. She looks so far afield that she cannot see the little duties lying to her hand, in the performance of which lies her best training for great and worthy deeds. Many a girl dreams of such an ideal as Florence Nightingale, and nevertheless shrieks and runs out of the room when her little brother cuts his hand with the carving-knife. What a scared, helpless creature she would be in a hospital! Another girl pictures herself a heroine of self-denial, giving

A girl's idea of usefulness.

up "all" for some one, while she is too lazy to run upstairs to fetch her mother's gloves, or too self-indulgent to read the money article in *The Times* to her father. She is not "faithful in small things," though she fully intends to excel in great. The ideal daughter is the unselfish, active, intelligent, and good-tempered girl, who thinks out what she can do to help her mother, to make life pleasanter for her father, and home happier for her brothers.

The ideal daughter.

Many girls think self-culture the first and greatest duty of all, but in thinking so, and in acting on the thought, they turn their backs upon real self-culture. Doing something for others, when we would rather be doing something for ourselves, goes further towards self-culture, in its highest and best sense, than reading the cleverest book ever written, or practising the most difficult music. There have been girls who, thinking it their duty, have refused to leave their parents, even to marry the man they love. This is usually a mistaken notion of "*fais ce que dois*," for it throws on the father and mother a terrible weight of obligation, never to be paid off, and even if they know nothing of the sacrifice at the time it is made, it is certain to come home to them sooner or later. Is it not Ruskin who declares that self-denial, when it is carried beyond the boundary of common sense, becomes

True self-culture.

an actual injury against those for whom it is practised? There is a deep truth in this.

Youth is not naturally self-denying. Human nature is strongly selfish, and when girls are young they have had little chance to oppose the strength of this inherent quality. Some girls, however, are much less selfish than others, while some are utterly spoilt! A doting mother is nothing more nor less than a selfish mother, who, *to please herself*, allows her daughter's faults to grow up unchecked. She fears to be firm, lest she should lose some of the affection she prizes. Could she only know that the child, at a very early age, is distinctly aware of this weakness and despises it, she would plainly see the awful mistake she is making. Children love best the mothers who are both firm and gentle. By a sort of instinct the young ones seem to be aware of the true selflessness that actuates the parent who battles with their early faults. It is not the foolishly indulgent mothers who win the warmest love from their girls. It is those who can temper justice with love. Girls soon know whether the mother is swayed by selfishness or actuated by principle, and, with very few exceptions, they follow in her steps.

About un-selfishness.

Could some of the happy lovers and happy husbands look back through the years at the long and patient training,

the loving care, that has resulted in
the complete realisation of
The home training. their brightest dreams—"My
queen! my queen!"—they
would find in them a guarantee for the
future. Girls who have not been spoiled
by over-indulgence, and who have been
taught to take a sane, calm, rational
view of all life's circumstances, are the
best helpmeets that man can have.
Such an one is a delightful companion,
with her cultivated mind and her ready
sympathies. She can enter into his
outside troubles in the battle of life,
and there is a fibre of strength in her
on which he may safely lean in the day
of disaster, should it come.

OUR SCHOOL-GIRLS.

MOTHERS of growing girls have many
an anxious hour. The young things feel
so bright, so strong, so full of
energy, that it is difficult for
them to listen to the voice of
prudent counsel which bids them take
care of themselves, and mothers often
give in when a word of warning is received with laughing heedlessness. And
how frequently they have to regret the
giving in ! When girls are growing
very fast, even if they keep up their
strength and look strong and well,
there is much risk in any over-fatigue.
The heart is sometimes outpaced by
the rest of the frame, and if care be not
taken there is a possibility of inducing
strain, which may result in permanent
mischief. Girls want to run, play sett
after sett of tennis, or go on pulling a
boat on the river when they are already
hot and tired, and it is only natural that
they should fancy that their capacity for
enjoyment is as inexhaustible as their
taste for it.

But the doctors will tell mothers
to restrain the young creatures from
damaging their health by over-exertion,

and if we fail to do so we may some day feel agonies of remorse. **Over-exertion.** It is easy enough to manage this so long as they are quite young and under our own eyes all day, but when school-time begins matters are very different. The spirit of emulation awakes, and the keenest anxiety to equal other girls in progress spurs on the young spirit. Teachers are anxious, too, and the mother often has to do battle on behalf of her daughter, not only with the school authorities, but with the girl herself. Firmness with both is the only method, and this in face of protests on one side and tears and expostulations on the other. The teachers think the mother "ridiculously fussy," and condole with the girl, stirring her up to rebellion in a most injudicious way; but after all the mother is in the right and must be firm. What is the use of class successes if they are won at the expense of health? And though scholarships are very pleasant things in more ways than one, they may cost too dear. If the money they save has to go in doctors' fees, of what earthly use are they?

At the same time mothers must not sacrifice the young ones to nervous or morbid fears, as some are inclined to do. The only way to be sure that precautions are really necessary is to have advice from a doctor, and if a girl is growing very quickly he is almost sure to say that she must not do too much.

As a rule girls spend far too many hours a day in study. School-days **Too much study.** come just when they are very busy growing, and it is also the time when habits are formed. With all these contradictory considerations influencing the mother, she is often afraid to trust her own judgment as to whether this or that course shall be pursued. If the girl is worked too hard she may become nervous or anæmic, and if she is allowed to rest too much she may grow up lazy and self-indulgent. So what is one to do? With our limited powers all we can do is to watch the growing daughters from day to day, and if they show any signs of failing energies, or of weakening health, at once take steps to lessen the number of hours devoted to study. At each succeeding term the school programme should be carefully gone through, with a view to seeing if the lessons that follow consecutively may not be too trying, and, if so, arrangements should be made with the head of the school to spare the girl a long run of monotonous subjects.

The school authorities, naturally enough, arrange the hours to suit themselves and their teachers, and sometimes with the result that a girl has to rush back to school after a hasty meal, her **Meal hours.** food actually doing her harm instead of good in consequence. It is in cases like this that the mother comes in—not always, you may be very sure, to the unmitigated delight of the teachers, or even of the girl herself ! In fact, the poor mother often gets blamed all round. The members of her own family are profuse in criticism, as a rule, of everything that she does in connection with her children. The best thing she can do is to ignore their opinion completely, for, whatever she does, she is sure to be blamed. If two diametrically opposite courses are open before her, whichever she chooses is sure to be condemned by somebody. It is the old story of the old man and his donkey. When it carried him the people found fault, and when he carried it they were as censorious as ever. We must just go the way our conscience points out, and present a stoical front to criticism. The philosophy embodied in the good old French motto comes to our aid : "*Fais ce que dois advienne que pourra.*"

It does wonders for a girl to lie down for even half an hour a day. But to lie sideways or crumpled up in the extraordinary fashion beloved of girls is of no use whatever. The shoulders must be flat, and the head not much raised. If a book is read the while it **The best way to rest.** must be held so that the eyes are wide open in reading ; the feet should be stretched out to their full length, so as to give as much rest to the muscles as possible. Girls run so tall nowadays that they need extra care, and it is the mothers who must see to it that they get it. On free mornings an extra half hour in bed will do no harm, but rather good ; and it should be always understood that this is an indulgence to be accepted as a boon for which gratitude is to be felt and expressed. To encourage young people to express gratitude is good for them.

Expressing thanks. It is strange, but true, that human nature is averse to express thanks with cordiality, and it is one of the marks of the well-bred girl that her thanks follow as naturally upon the act that elicits them as if the two were cause and effect.

Some of the high schools offer so many facilities in the various departments of education that the danger is of tremendously overworking the girls. One of whom I knew was at work from nine a.m. till half-past eight at night five days in the week, and from nine till two on Saturdays. The only exercise that she had was in her daily walk to and from school—once in the morning and again after lunch—and her only recreation was an occasional romp with her small brothers and sisters in the nursery. The girl broke down, as any one might safely have predicted that she would, and her costly education was entirely thrown away, for by the time that she was well enough to resume study she had forgotten all that she had learned.

Dangers of High Schools.

There is another danger connected with overdoing study in the time of girlhood that must not be overlooked.

OUR SCHOOL-GIRLS.

It is that of wearying young people with books, and so tiring Bad training. them that they never want to open one on a serious subject after they have left school-days behind them. To do this is to lose for them one of the greatest pleasures of life. Education, rightly understood, is a drawing out, not a crowding in. The best education consists in developing the powers and eliciting the bent of the mind, and laying a foundation for future culture. To speak of any girl's education as being "finished" is tantamount to speaking of a scaffolding as being finished, preparatory to the real work being begun. In after life comes the true work, and circumstances have much to do in guiding it. There is, therefore, no reason that growing girls should be overburdened with ologies and isms. French and German they must learn ; drawing, if they have a special taste for it, and the piano, on the same terms. It is utter waste to teach some girls to play on the piano, and the idea that it is a necessary part of polite education is now rapidly disappearing from the cultured classes of society. Simplification in every branch is one of the safest rules of life, and this applies as much to the programme of a girl's existence as to that of her mother.

There is no doubt that, in a great degree, the improvement in the physique of English girls is largely due to the enlightened ideas of their parents on subjects connected with **Hygiene and sanitation.** hygiene and sanitation. The nation is wonderfully improved on these matters, during the last fifteen years, and it is at last beginning to be understood that a perfectly sound body is necessary to a perfectly healthy and capable mind. If girls are encouraged to place the culture of the mind not only before, but in opposition to, that of the body, they must be consequent sufferers—if not in girlhood, at some later period ; and may bequeath suffering to others. So, mothers, be advised in time, and let girlhood be the healthy, happy, sunny time that Nature intended it to be. Our girls are young but once, and it is not for long. The cares of life will soon enough cloud over their brightness. Do not allow overwork or long hours to shadow the irrecoverable springtime.

WHAT ABOUT SEWING?

SOME of the very advanced and extremely superior women of the present day are strenuously opposed to the teaching of needlework in girls' schools and colleges. A mere handicraft should be beneath the notice of highly intellectual human beings, and should be left to those whose intelligence is of a lower order. That is their creed. I am glad to see that one of the cleverest and most learned women of the time, Mrs. Bryant, D.Sc., advocates, though in a half-hearted and semi-apologetic fashion, the teaching of needlework to girls receiving the higher education. She thinks that, just as a man is a somewhat incomplete person if he cannot make himself useful with a hammer, a plane, and a saw, a woman who cannot sew is equally an anomaly. The man who wants a rent in his glove stitched would be likely to regard her as much more so. But I must not, from this, be understood as advocating the accomplishment of sewing merely with a view to the repair of men's sartorial damages.

The prejudice against sewing.

A word in its favour.

25

This would be to invoke indeed the wrath of the superior woman, who thinks it degradation to stoop to all the sweet, old-fashioned, housewifely uses and despises her gentler sisters who delight in making home comfortable and life smooth for those who dwell with her.

One of the best and foremost reasons for teaching sewing to girls is the training it involves. Our wonder-

The training it involves. ful finger-tips have within them possibilities which oftentimes lie dormant throughout a whole lifetime for the want of education. The Great Genius who made them gave them a capacity of delicate, sensitive touch, which is blurred and lost when not encouraged and promoted. The hands that can wield a needle with celerity and skill have necessarily received a training that tells for them in many another way besides mere sewing. The servant who sews well is the one who breaks fewest things. She has learned to use her finger-tips. The clumsy woman who uses brute force in dealing with the most delicate articles, and is constantly smashing and damaging something or other is she who has never been taught to sew, or in some way had manual training. The value of this development of finger-training is greater than at first sight

Its moral value. might be imagined. Through the hands the mind and character are influenced. Patience progresses while the diligent little fingers of the child are at work, conquering difficulties gradually and achieving skill day after day with a continued progression towards perfection. The lesson in perseverance is a fine one, and no less valuable is the necessary exertion in self-control, which soon becomes a habit and works wonders in producing repose of manner. This last may not be a particularly valuable quality, but it is a delightful one in this restless age, when few people seem able to settle down for more than half an hour at a time, even to the agreeable occupation of reading.

It may seem exaggerated to attribute so much to the mere learning to sew ; but a little examination into the matter will prove to the thoughtful that there is something in it. Any man, for instance, who has learned even a little carpentering, will admit that the effect on his mind and character of perfecting himself in any one of the necessary processes was distinctly good. It promotes clearness of thought, banishing that vague slovenliness of ideas which is analogous to the ragged edges of a frayed garment. To many an uneducated worker the acquirement of skill in some handicraft has brought with it an upward influence that has led him far in the direction of self-improvement.

And mental effect.

But there must be moderation in it. Many an intellectual life has been killed by intemperate sewing. It was the

27

creed of our grandmothers that everything else for girls was idling.

Moderation.

Long seams were regarded
as the business of young lives, and to be
unable to sew well as a disgrace. Harriet
Martineau tells us all about it in her
" Household Education." She says, " I
believe it is now generally

**Harriet
Martineau
on overdoing
it.**

agreed, among those who
know best, that the practice of
sewing has been carried much
too far for health, even in houses where
there is no poverty or pressure of any
kind. No one can well be more fond
of sewing than I am ; and few, except
professional sempstresses, have done
more of it ; and my testimony is that it
is a most hurtful occupation, except
where great moderation is observed. I
think it is not so much the sitting and
stooping posture as the incessant monotonous action and position of the arms
that causes such wear and tear. Whatever it may be, there is something in
prolonged sewing which is remarkably
exhausting to the strength, and irritating
beyond endurance to the nerves. The
censorious gossip, during sewing, which
was the bane of our youth," she adds,
" wasted more of our precious youthful
powers and dispositions than any re-
pentance and amendment in after life
could repair."

In the exhibition of " Fair Children,"
held at the Grafton Gallery some seasons
since, there was a whole case full of
cruel samplers, which must have made

many a young child miserable. Because,
you know, it is not only the
Those bar-barous samplers. work that is visible that went
into them! There were the
tedious and endless unpickings
when mistakes were made, causing
bitter tears of woe to rise in childish
eyes. "You shall stay in, Araminta,
until you get it right." And outside was
the sun shining, the birds were singing,
the meadows full of hay, and the other
children romping and shouting. Poor
Araminta! There was her
Poor Araminta. name embroidered on one of
the most barbarous of those
dreadful samplers; one with a double
border, the outer one in circles, the
inner in vandykes. The stitches in each
had to be counted, and every one
crossed in the same direction. And Araminta was aged seven! There it was,
at the end of her sampler, "Araminta
Paget. Her sampler. Aged seven."
Composition ambiguous, but meaning
clear. Well, perhaps Araminta learned
to love her fine marking, and passed
many a happy hour singing to herself
over her embroidery frame; but it is
good to remember that the old tyranny
of the needle is past and gone. The
invention of the sewing-machine has
been to women one of the very greatest
blessings of our dear Queen's most
beneficent reign. I am not sure that it
was not the real means of introducing
many others, legal and educational.

When Caddy Jellaby remarked,

"Africa's a beast!" she was but unconsciously paraphrasing an
Berlin
woolwork.
expression of opinion familiar
enough to her contemporaries.
How many thousands of girls in those
old days have declared, "Berlin wool's
a bother!" And so, indeed, it was.
To be able to do what was then called
"fancy work" was almost sufficient
accomplishment for the young women
of the middle classes of those days.
Cushions, chair furniture, slippers, and
even pictures were produced in this
despotic cross-stitch, varied occasionally by a finer and more difficult variety
called tent-stitch; and so far from
employing fancy or imagination, every
row had to be diligently counted—so
many brown stitches, so many green, so
many red, &c. I have seen hearthrugs
worked in this way with Berlin wool in
impossibly huge flowers, and the fender-
stool was a great favourite in those old
days, often made prickly with white
beads, in which recumbent lilies were
delineated. Fire screens of the hanging
banner pattern were esteemed as great
ornaments, and I believe I once heard
of a carpet worked in sections by an
ambitious party of ladies, and afterwards joined together.

But who wastes time over fancy work
now? Only a small minority of women,
I fancy. There is a market
Waste
of time.
for beautiful sewing and for
fine embroideries, but as for
futile and inartistic chairbacks and their

30

tribe, their day is done. The exquisite Church embroideries bring in fair incomes to those skilled in that class of work; but there is no longer any demand for the home-made lace that occupied half the waking hours of many a woman's life in the sixties and seventies. That nightmare is over. But let us hope that skill with the needle will never be despised among gentlewomen. To put it on the very lowest ground, it is a marvellous economy to be able to sew. If one had to pay for every little repair in one's garments, as men have, it would cost a large sum of

The policy and sentiment of the matter. money in every year, for our dresses are not so durable as men's coats. And even the richest of women can never be absolutely certain that she will not one day be poor. "Nothing is certain except that nothing is certain," and the changes of this troublesome world are capable of anything. But, apart from motives of policy, the accomplishment of sewing is a part of refined femininity. And think of the pleasure that women would lose without it. Think of the thoughts sewn into the beautiful little garments fashioned for the babies—the hopes and fears, the love and tenderness, and the far outlook into the future that comes with mother-love. All these are stitched in with the flying needle; and who would be without these long, long thoughts? To be able to sew is utilitarian. It is also conducive to happiness.

31

MOTHERS AND SONS.

A "PUBLIC SCHOOLMAN" once said,
"If a mother would only harden her
boys a little, send them
away to a private school at
ten and afterwards to a
public school, there would then be no
complaints of being teased." There is
no doubt that mothers do often err on
the side of softness, as any one of us
can see by the number of spoiled
children we meet in any given twenty-
four hours. Widows' sons are only too
often intolerably conceited, spoilt with
indulgence, and apt to repay their
mother's tenderness by breaking her
heart. She makes life so smooth for
them that they can never refuse themselves anything, and sometimes their
whole lives are spoiled by their mother's
weakness, which, in its turn, is only a
form of self-indulgence. Such a boy,
on entering a public school, meets with
no mercy, but the discipline is just
what he needs to knock the nonsense
out of him and make him a man, not a
namby-pamby noodle.

But, having acknowledged that the
mother is often to blame, let us look at

On
spoiling boys.

32

the other side of the shield. The boy of ten who is sent away from home to a private school finds that he has to take absolutely new views of life in almost every particular. Perplexed by the new horizon, the novel atmosphere, and with his young heart aching for home tenderness and affection, he is assisted in adjusting himself to his altered circumstances by bullying and sneers. The treatment is on all fours with that of " hitting a man when he is down," a practice which is supposed to be repugnant to all British notions of honour and fair play. When a horse falls under a heavy load in the slippery streets, and the driver whips, slashes, and swears at the poor brute, a murmur of indignation goes up from the spectators. But no one sympathises with the boy, who dare not give the faintest sign of the suffering he feels. The injustice of it all is often what rankles most deeply. There are many mothers who train their boys to a fine sense of honour, derived from a much higher source than that which seems to inspire the average schoolboy, and the ordinary man of the world into whom the boy develops. His attitude to his fellow-creatures is one of comradeship, and kindly feeling, when he leaves his mother's side. Who shall say what storms of rancorous hate and bitter loathing pass over the young soul in the boy's first term at school ? His sense

First days at school.

3

of injustice becomes distorted for life,
under such a system as that described
in the following.

" The old *régime* when ' kids' blacked
boots, cooked potatoes and pies, made
coffee or cocoa for the bigger
boys, when we had to 'fag'
at the fives' courts and cricket nets, and
got 'fives batted,' or ' cricket stumped,'
if we stopped the balls badly. We enjoyed the pleasures of being tossed in a
blanket, or having our faces blackened
with the bottom of a saucepan taken off
the fire, and of having our trousers
rolled above our knees and our calves
roasted before the fire. We learnt by
experience that, although the cricket
ball chastised us with whips, W.'s hands
chastised us with scorpions, and that
W.'s little finger was thicker than the
cricket ball. We played the old-
fashioned Rugby : ' hacked' a fellow
over instead of ' collaring' him when he
ran, and, instead of ' working out' the
ball in the scrimmage, we ' hacked'
each other's shins in what was then
called the ' gutter.' Two or three days
before the match we used to get the
shoemaker to put new soles on our
boots, and to make the toe points of
the soles project, so that we might
make our 'hacks' all the more stinging."

This is a picture of public schools
which must make many a mother's
heart ache for her boy. And are not
mothers meant for softness and tenderness ? That they sometimes let them-

By a " fag."

34

selves fall into the extreme of weak and backboneless indulgence does not prove that mothers are not meant for gentleness and sympathy in the lives of their sons. They know well that school life is the only way of hardening boys against the time when they have to do battle with the world. But the hardening process need not, and should not, imply the coarsening and toughening of all that is meant to be delicately sensitive, sympathetic, and generously responsive.

It is true that some splendid men are turned out by public schools. The system is a good one, but it has been carried to a dangerous extreme. The fine fellows who have emerged unharmed are fine fellows in spite of all that was dangerous, not because of it. How many fine fellows has it ruined? Such treatment is destructive of candour, sincerity, frankness, generosity, simplicity, and often of truthfulness itself. The principle that might is right is dead against the law of the land, but it seems to rule in our public schools, where the big bully—usually a coward at heart—makes the lives of young boys wretched. The love of cruelty innate in such despotic natures is developed to the utmost degree by such favourable circumstances, and those over whom he tyrannises become sly, secretive, and hypocritical.

The old adage says that if there were

35

no women in the world the men would
all be brutes; and if there

The shadow that may not pass. were no men the women
would all be fools. The
mother's ideal school might
be very far indeed from a perfect one,
but, as things are, one of the bitterest
of her griefs is when she has to send
her gentle, affectionate, pure-minded
and open-souled little lad to school.
She knows well that he will have to
struggle alone through the dark days of
initiation into school life, its cheap and
shallow cynicism, its endless injustices,
and its darker shadows than any that
have been referred to. The mother
knows she is losing her boy. She will
never again read his thoughts as an
open book. She casts her bread upon
the waters, and may, or may not,
receive it after many days. Her boy
may never again be the candid, gentle,
bright-spirited being whose companionship was delightful to her. His con-
fidence may never again be hers, and
she knows better than to force it, or
even invite it with loving insistence. If
he ever again opens his mind to her it
will be as naturally as the dove returned
to the ark. But the cloud of school
life must come between them first.
And it is often a black one.

This is supposed to be a Christian
land; but at how many public schools
in England does a small boy dare to
kneel and say his nightly prayer as he
did at home? Sometimes a strong and

earnest spirit among the bigger boys succeeds in living the higher life, even at school, where all traditions are dead against active religion, as the small boy who essays such a course soon finds to his cost. The mother's ideal school would be one in which the young spirit might be free to lay some of the burden of school life at the feet of the Great Friend. But "cant," as any sign of religious feeling is called at school, is regarded as a thing to be driven out by sneers and gibes, flickings with a damp towel, and—worse than all—hideous references to holy things and to the mother who taught them. Everything that is pure and true seems to be sullied and robbed of truth and goodness, and there appears to be nothing left for the boy to cling to while his universe is in a whirl, the things he held sacred desecrated, and a stream of lurid light thrown upon the seamy side of life so carefully concealed from him at home.

The spiritual life.

OUR CLEVER CHILDREN.

MR. ANDREW LANG disputes Dr. Johnson's definition of genius as "an infinite capacity for taking *What is genius?* pains," and seem to make out a good case for doing so. Mr. Lang's own definition is "an unmeasured capacity for doing things without taking pains." What a width of worlds lies between the two conceptions! I suppose the real truth is that genius is indefinable, and so varied in character as to escape all attempts at classification. But there it is, to be reckoned with, and when the mother goes into the nursery and looks round at all the dear little people there, she can no more guess if any of them is going to be a genius than she can tell what Destiny has in store for them in the way of aches and pains and accidents. Some of the stupid ones are as likely to turn out geniuses as the bright and clever. Sir *Sir Walter Scott.* Walter Scott was a dull boy at school. There were things he could never learn. He loathed figures, and it is pathetic to remember what a hideous part they played in his hard-worked life. As to his attempts at poetry, they were very much in the rough at this early age, but he loved other people's poetry so much that his mind was compact of it. He could reel it off by the furlong. He was always lovable, and his laugh was so hearty that it could often be heard long before the laugher came in sight.

But genius is not always lovable. In this way it is frequently a terrible trial to its possessor, especially in the days of childhood, when subjugation to the domestic powers often involves a considerable amount of real suffering. Read Hans Andersen's "Ugly Duckling" in this sense, and you have some idea of the intense loneliness of a brilliant mind in early days, when no one understands it, and when every effort towards expression is checked and thwarted, every attempt at development coerced. Later on, when genius will out, and shines resplendent, seen and recognised of all men, what agonies of self-reproach do parents feel! What would they not give to have the time over again wherein they might, with comprehension added, soothe and sustain the tried young spirit, solacing it with kindness and giving it the balm of sympathy and tenderness. "If I had only known," say the mothers, who treated the absorption and aloofness of their clever children as sullenness and bad-temper, and

"If I had only known."

allowed themselves to grow apart from the lonely young spirit, which needed more than most the loving kindness of home and friends. For genius

The loneliness of genius.

is essentially solitary. There are depths and heights in the inner consciousness of many a child of seven that are far beyond the view of millions of educated adults. Shallowness is the rule ; a comfortable shallowness, which, unknowing of better things, measures all other minds with its own limited plummet line, and can conceive of no deeper depth. How could it ? And hence those solitudes in which the spirit wanders lonely, yet longing for companionship. A thirst is ever on it for a comprehending sympathy, and when the young soul looks appealingly out at us, through wistful eyes, it has no plainer language. It asks for bread, and we give it a stone.

And we put it all down to sulks ! —unguessing of the tumult going on within the teeming brain and

Misunderstood !

the starved heart. Mothers, be gentle with young ones you cannot understand. You little know what a dagger lies hidden in the sentence so often heard : " Well, you *are* queer. I can't understand you." And you would be astonished if you could know how early some souls realise their own loneliness. A child of tender years soon learns its reticences. It almost intuitively feels the lack of response in others, and expression is soon checked of all that lies behind the mere commonplaces of existence.

What does Thackeray say? "To what mortal ear could I tell all, if I had a mind? Or who could understand all?" And another writer expresses a similar idea: "There are natures which ever must be silent to other natures, because there is no common language between them. In the same house, at the same board, sharing the same pillow, even, are those for ever strangers and foreigners, whose whole stock of intercourse is limited to a few brief phrases on the commonest material wants of life, and who, as soon as they try to go further, have no words that are mutually understood."

And again Thackeray, this time in "Vanity Fair," as before in "Pendennis": "To how many people can any one tell all? Who will be open when there is no sympathy, or has call to speak to those who never can understand?"

If mothers would only understand that this conscious aloofness begins early in some natures—almost incredibly early—they would be happier in their clever children and would make them happier too. There comes a moment when the young mind that has lain clear and open as a book before one's eyes enwraps itself in a misty veil, and enters into the silent solitude which every human being finds within his own nature. And the mother, unguessing, is hurt and repelled, though she should be well aware that the time must come when the youthful soul must enter upon its inheritance of individuality, and separate itself and stand apart. It is at this momentous time that affection is most deeply needed, with a craving and a yearning that cannot be expressed; and yet this is the moment when the mother too often turns away, disappointed and chilled by the unwonted reticence her child displays. She has yet to learn that human affection is a wingless thing, and cannot follow the far flights of the untrammelled spirit. It is well for

Recognising our limitations. mothers to recognise their limitations, and to realise that there may be far more in her child's mind than was ever dreamed of by herself. If she fails to do this, she will chill back the love that lies, warm as ever, behind the incomprehensible reserve wherewith the youthful spirit wraps itself while it learns what all this inner tumult means. It is a trying time for both parent and son or daughter, and the only thing to keep firm hold of is the love that holds the two together. It is more important than ever at this parting of the ways, though it may seem to be disregarded. There will surely be a call upon it when the inner solitudes are found immeasurable, and when the spirit, almost affrighted at its own illimitable possibilities, turns back to the dear human hand and the loving glance and word that sufficed it always until now.

Mothers must play a waiting game in these matters. Expostulation is worse than useless, only puzzling. Demands for explanation are worse than purposeless. Both tend to still further harass a perplexed mind. Only patience is recommendable, and always love, and plenty of it, for the young sons and daughters. They may not seem to need it, and may even appear to be indifferent to it ; but it is good for them to know that when they want it, as they very surely will, it is there for them. These doves that return to the ark are often very weary, and long for rest and comfort. Too often they find coldness and repulsion.

The need of patience.

Mr. Andrew Lang says that the future genius is often violent, ferocious, fond of solitude, disagreeable in society. And how is the mother to divine from these qualities a budding poet or a master of men ? For there are crowds of disagreeable, rude boys to be found on every hand. Intuitive knowledge would be desirable on this point, but we cannot have it, and without it the only thing to do is to correct faults vigorously, but never to discontinue affection.

The young genius.

43

Many parents are good at one or other, but it is the few who can manage both. Gentleness is such a delightful quality that it is often encouraged and applauded at the expense of firmness ; and the moral courage necessary for exercising the latter remains untrained, and soon dies out for want of care. For this kind of courage only needs practice, like patience and the piano, and, fortunately, each effort makes it easier. Great, rough boys are wonderfully amenable to gentleness when they know that firmness lies behind it. Lacking that, it is regarded as "softness," and played upon for their own purposes. It is deplorable to see the way the boys are treated in some families. They are noisy and ill-mannered, it is true ; but they would improve if they could only be gently borne with, instead of being made to feel as if they were nuisances and interlopers. They may never be geniuses, but for all that they have a right to consideration in the only home they know. And they do not always get it. Listen to the lament of one of them :—

About gentleness.

"What can a boy do, and where can a boy stay,
　If he always is told to get out of the way ?
　　He cannot sit here, and he mustn't stand there,
　　The cushions that cover that gaily-decked chair
Were put there, of course, to be seen and admired ;
A boy has no business to feel a bit tired.
The beautiful carpets with blossom and bloom

The Boy's Lament.

OUR CLEVER CHILDREN.

On the floor of the tempting and light-shaded
    room,
Are not made to be walked on—at least, not by
    boys.
The house is no place, anyway, for their noise.

There's a place for the boys.   They will find it
    somewhere,
And if our own homes are too daintily fair
For the touch of their fingers, the tread of their
    feet,
They'll find it, and find it, alas ! in the street,
'Mid the gildings of sin and the glitter of vice ;
And with heartaches and longings we pay a dear
    price
For the getting of gain that our lifetime employs
If we fail in providing a place for our boys.

Though our souls may be vexed with the prob-
    lems of life,
And worn with besetments and toiling and strife,
Our hearts will keep younger—your tired heart
    and mine—
If we give them a place in our innermost shrine ;
And till life's latest hour 'twill be one of our joys
That we keep a small corner—a place for the
    boys."

ULTRA-TIDINESS.

WE have all heard of the fortunate lady whose "very failings leaned to virtue's side." Is there a converse to her? Do none of our virtues lean to vice's side? I think I could enumerate a few, but for the moment the vicious side of tidiness *The vicious side of tidiness.* is so strongly borne in upon me that I need go no further afield. Tidiness is delightful, meritorious, indispensable, admirable, estimable, praiseworthy, politic, and most precious. Untidiness is execrable, reprehensible, unseemly, and quite detestable. It is first cousin to uncleanliness, and is the mother of much domestic warfare. Tidiness is a virtue, indeed, but when carried to an extreme it becomes actually a disagreeable quality. My first impression to that effect was imbibed at the early age of nine, when I was sent to a boarding school. Separated from home and all familiar faces, I had a miserable heartache, even in the reception-room, but the sight of the awful tidiness of the dormitory chilled me to the very soul. The white walls, white beds, boarded floor, with its strips of carpet in a sad

monotone of tint, gave me my first definite sensation of the mean-
Tyrannical cleanliness. ing of the word "bleak."
And ever after, when re-
turned to school from the holidays, I
dreaded the moment of entering that
long dormitory, where tidiness and
cleanliness reigned rampant, like
tyrants, instead of inviting, like the
friendly, comfortable things they really
are.

I know a mother who will not allow
her children to have toys, " because they
are always lying about." Well, toys
are a very good means of teaching
children tidiness ; but the true mother-
heart must be lacking when
Selfish neatness. the young ones are robbed
of their childish joys for so
selfish a reason. Childhood lasts so
short a time, and can be so happy.
Why curtail its little blisses ? Just a
few toys are more productive of
pleasure than the plethora which so
many nurseries display nowadays. And
why should tidiness forbid a few ?

For my part I like to see a battered
old doll knocking about in the drawing-
room of my friends. Generally armless,
sometimes legless, occasionally head-
less, that doll becomes an enchanted
spring of poetry when its small pro-
prietress comes in and takes it up,
loving it deeply and warmly in spite of
its painful ugliness, its damaged condition, and general want of charm. Is
not that what love does for us all ?

47

Ignoring our faults, it throws its glamour over us, and gives us what enriches the donor as well as the recipient—the most precious thing on earth.

The mother who deprives her small daughter of a doll sacrifices more than she knows to the demon of tidiness, and she robs herself of much delight. The consultations about dolly's health are often funny enough. The discussions about the wax and bran-stuffed thing's temper and naughtiness give many a peep into those departments of the child's own nature, afford many a clue to the best method of treating them, and are, besides, amusing beyond expression. And where is poor Tommy, among boys, without his gun, his sword, and pistol ? He is despised of his peers, and almost despises himself in consequence. It is bad for Tommy, very bad. Yes ; tidiness can be very selfish. One can scarcely pardon the mothers who allow it to interfere with home joys.

About dolly.

I know people who object to flowers in the house because "they are so messy." They droop and die indeed. 'Tis a true indictment, but they are worth some trouble, are they not ? Ultra-tidiness would banish them, and some of us would willingly be banished with them from the realms so ruled. Flowers do not last nearly so long when housed by persons of this sort as

"Those messy flowers."

with those who love them, tend them
daily, cherish them with warmest care,
anticipate their needs, as only love can
do, and attract from them some subtle,
scarcely comprehensible, sympathy that
prolongs the existence of these exquisite, innocent things, whose companionship means so much to man.

The æsthetes in their day revelled in
untidiness. They made a cult of it, and
"Tone." in their worship included a
leaning towards dirt, which
they canonised under the name of
"Tone." Many of them permitted
even their faces to acquire tone by this
means, which was carrying the thing too
far. But they did much for succeeding
generations in banishing a too pronounced neatness from dress and the
home. Has not the influence of the
æsthete delivered us from the
The grateful terrible propriety of chairs
shade of the
æsthete. ranged along the wall, piano
to match, and the centre-table,
with its unalterable rigidity of central
ornament and rim of book and vase in
conic sectional immutability ?

Oh, it was all most beautifully tidy,
but do, for a moment, recall it and
compare it with the drawing-room of
to-day. I do not mean the dusty litter
of dilapidated draperies and orgie of
over-crowded ornament to be found in
some houses, but to the sane, yet
artistic arrangement of table and lamp,
piano and pottery, palm and vase,
clustering fern and glowing blossom or

snowy flower, to be seen in thousands of English homes at the present hour. Here tidiness is not absent, but its rigours are avoided. Its essence is extracted, while its needless extremes —its suburbs, as it were—are totally ignored. We have learned how to be clean, yet decorative, in our homes and our costume, to distinguish between severity and simplicity, and, so far, good. But the point is that tidiness should not overcome us to the hurt of others, and consequently our own. If husbands persist in leaving a trail of newspapers all over the house, something after the fashion of the " hare " in a paper-chase, let us calmly fold them and assuage our inner revolt as best we may. If the children scatter their toys about, we can make them put them tidily away, and that is more than we can manage with their fathers ! But to be too acutely tidy leads to friction and the development of that " incompatibility of temper" which seems to be quite a modern disease, to judge from the very numerous instances of it that come before the public notice.

A word to the wise.

GOOD MANNERS AT HOME.

IT is usually the wife and mother who sets the key of behaviour in the home.

Woman's influence in the home. If she is loud and rough, her servants and her children will follow suit. If she is gentle, kindly, and patient, her example will exercise a subtle influence on even the noisest of her domestics. Sometimes, when a man has married beneath him, his first disillusionment, after the glamour of his love is past, is caused by the *brusquerie* of the uneducated and ill-trained wife. And, on the other hand, when a girl or woman has married beneath her own class— run away with a handsome groom or become the wife of a good-looking jockey—her domestic experiences are calculated to be her severest punishment. A relative of one such misguided girl, having visited her in her married home, said afterwards to a friend : " His manners at table, my dear, are simply frightful, but they compare agreeably with his behaviour anywhere else, for he neither talks nor swears when he is eating." What a life-companion for a well-bred girl ! Should the husband have any gentleness or goodness stowed away within him, he is sure to improve as time goes on. His wife is an education to him, but at such a tremendous cost to herself as to be absolutely incalculable.

In ordinary cases, however, it is the wife who is responsible for the home manners. And, oh ! what a **Where** difference they make ! In **manners** **are absent.** some families there is a constant jar and fret of sulks and little tempers. Politeness among the members is wholly ignored. Each one says the first disagreeable thing that occurs to him, and the others warmly follow suit. The habit grows on all, and the result is a state of things that makes the gentle-minded among the inmates of the home long for peace and rest, and seize the first opportunity of leaving it. And it is so easy, after all, to initiate a far different and more agreeable state of things. The young ones can be trained to gentleness and good manners, to self-control under provocation, and to the daily practice of those small acts of self-denial, self-control, and true courtesy, which do so much towards building up conditions of home happiness.

There are, of course, churlish natures which nothing could ever influence in the direction of true polite- **Churlish** ness, which always means **natures.** self-effacement to a certain extent. It is of such as these that a

52

student of human nature has said, "*Grattez le Russe, et vous trouvez le Tartare.*" Would that such beings were confined to Russia ! How happy would other countries be in their absence ! The smallest touch to their vanity, their enormously developed self-love, their triumphant self-conceit, robs them in a moment of any surface polish they may ever have acquired. As a breath upon a mirror dulls its brightness, and renders it useless for

Their rampant egotism. the purposes for which it is made, so does the merest suggestion or shadow of a shade of blame or criticism dull the touchy human subject, for a day, for a week, perhaps longer, rendering him or her unfit for ordinary social intercourse The egotism of such an one is ever rampant. It pervades his atmosphere, so that one can touch and hurt it from afar, with the most genuine absence of any intention to do so.

Oh, how disagreeable they are ! What cloudy blackness they spread over the home ! How they kill

Their presence a blight. the little joys and blisses that might otherwise surround the domestic hearth, giving human creatures solace for much suffering ! And, worse still, how completely they destroy the affection that might be theirs, if only they could unwrap themselves from the envelope of self in which they are enshrouded. No love, not even the strongest, can sustain itself

53

against years of brutal roughness, inter-
mittent it is true, but ever imminent.
For who can tell how innocently or
unconsciously one may wound the
outrageous self-conceit of one of these?
Martyrs in their own idea, they offer a
spectacle to gods and men which, could
they but see it with clearness in its true
aspect, would be so mortifying and
humiliating that it would convey a
highly salutary lesson. But they can
never see anything in its true light that
is connected with themselves. If love
is blind, what on earth is self-love?

But fortunately these dreadful people
are comparatively rare; and the majority
of English homes—thousands
A brighter picture. and thousands of them, thank
God!—are abodes of peace
and love, refuges from the cares of business and the coldness of the outer world.
The gentle courtesies of look and
manner are not reserved for strangers,
but freely dispensed in the domestic
circle. The smile, the word of sympathy
spoken in season, whether in the happiness or troubles of the others, the
thoughtfulness translated into actions
of kindly care for the well-being of all
within the house; all these are of almost
angelic import in daily life. One is
inclined to deify gentleness and the
sweet humility that is never exacting
when one realises how immensely they
act and re-act on home-life. It is,
perhaps, possible to rate them too
highly; but there are moments in

which they appear to be virtues of the very first order.

It is the mother's duty to teach children to behave well at home and elsewhere. Too often she fails in it, and the young ones are unruly. The great lesson of obedience has not been learned ; not even begun. And yet it means so much that is beyond and above mere obedience ! It is the beginning of moral training. It is like the mastering of the clefs and notes in music. That done, the learner may teach himself. Left undone, there is nothing but discord to be evolved from his best efforts.

The mother's duty to her children.

Fathers have not the same chance of spoiling the children. When they do, they chiefly incline to pet the girls. Mothers prefer, as a rule, to spoil the boys ; and many a wife owes half her married misery to the injudicious years of misrule in which her husband's boyhood was passed. Even now the girls are taught in many a nursery to give up at once anything that the boys may wish for. Is it not true ? And, being true, is it surprising that the age of chivalry is fading, fading ? And often, in Nursery-land, there is a tyrant girl. That tyrant girl, generally the eldest child, rules the little ones with a rod of iron, supplies the lacking discipline of parents with a terrorism which is founded on no principles of order or

Tyrants of Nursery-land.

of justice, and nourishes in infant breasts a like sentiment of tyranny to her own, that of the trampled slave who waits only for opportunity to be tyrant in his turn. That is what the carelessness of elders does in the nursery !

But the gentle firmness of the ideal house-ruler is as genially expansive as the warm southern airs that come in April, and make us forget, in a moment, the long bitterness of winter. If every one is not happy in the homes where it is to be found, at least every one has a chance of happiness. There is a wonderful solace in even the superficial sweetness of politeness in such a home. The stranger within its gates is at once aware of a balmy moral atmosphere, from which harsh words, frowning looks, recriminations, scowls, sulks, and all their kin are wholly banished, and where the amenities of life are at least as much studied as its more substantial needs. Has not Solomon himself given us a precedent for according more importance to the former than to the latter ? Has he not told us that— "Better is the dinner of herbs where love is than the stalled ox and hatred therewith " ?

The home of the ideal house-ruler.

ARE WOMEN COWARDS?

Has any one ever met, in real life, the woman who screams and jumps on a chair at the sight of a mouse? The old, old story. I have never heard of her out of the servants' hall, where ladies' maids appear to carry on the traditions of sensibility kept up by their betters two or three generations since, when nerves, swoonings, and burnt feathers played a prominent part in the lives of fashionable women. A little mouse has nothing terrible about it, vermin though it be in strict classification. Now, if it had been a rat! Or a blackbeetle! A large, long-legged, rattling cockroach! Truly, these are awesome things, and even the strongest-minded of women hate the sight of them. Very few women, I take it, are afraid of mice. And yet, as the world rolls on, that little story of a small grey mouse and screeching women will re-appear again and again, dressed up in fresh fancy costumes, when news is scarce and a corner of the paper has to be filled up.

But though we can watch with interest and amusement, and a sort of

kindly feeling, the actions of a mouse,
we are sad cowards all the
Are we moral cowards? same. Some of us are physi-
cally cowardly, though by no
means all ; but very few of us
are morally brave. I heard a sermon not
long ago on moral cowardice as shown
in the home. And who shall deny that
it is very, very difficult to obey the old
dictum : " *Fais ce que dois, advienne que
pourra*," and to deal faithfully with the
members of the home circle, from pater-
familias himself down to the little maid
in the basement territory ? The responsibility of the whole matter lies with
the wife and mother, involving many a
hard task, many a battle fought against
the secret shrinking from giving pain,
or causing disappointment, or rousing
temper. How difficult it
The children. is to refuse some pleasure
to the children we love, be-
cause it is injudicious for them, and
how fatally easy to give in weakly, and
prove ourselves cowardly ! And sometimes the punishment comes quickly :
" Oh, if I had only been firm, all this
might have been prevented !" we cry
in pain and sorrow when all the evil
consequences we had dimly foreseen
have become actual fact. Some of us
are so afraid that the children will
love us less if we interfere
One need not fear to be brave. with their childish joys and
pleasures. But, after all, this
need not be taken into account, for the youngsters possess a
58

divining crystal in their own clear thoughts, and know well when Love is at the helm. They can discern in a moment whether an arbitrary self-will dictates the course of things or that single-minded affection that seeks the truest good of those who are in its charge. They will not love us less, but more, as time goes on.

Besides, it is ignoble to be influenced by consequences that may result to ourselves, even possible loss of affection, the only earthly thing that is worth living for. "*Advienne que pourra*" are the grand old words.

A friend of mine, whose husband became a drunkard, told me that the most difficult thing she had ever done in her life was to remonstrate with him when he first began to drink too much. It was a clear duty, and she did it, but it required the summoning up of all her fortitude, as some who read these words may know but too well from their own experience. " When I began," she told me, " my knees trembled, and at last I shook as if I had been in an ague. It was quite dreadful to me to speak to him, and yet he took it as though I were out of temper, and merely shrewish." " And did it do any good ? " I asked, and she told me that he was better for a few weeks, and seemed to be struggling against the love of drink, but that after a couple of months things were as bad as ever again.

A difficult task.

I do not know any one possessed of
sufficient moral courage to deal faithfully
with their friends and relatives
on the subject of objection-
able little ways in eating or
drinking, or in the hundred
and one little actions of daily life. We
endure silently the sight of excessively
disagreeable habits rather than risk
giving mortal offence. In fact, we are
sad cowards. " How dreadful it is to
sit opposite So-and-so when he is eating," says one member of the family to
another. " He ought to be told about
it." " Oh, I couldn't ! I simply could
not," is the instant reply, and the other
echoes, " Nor I. Not for worlds !" And
So-and-so goes on in his ugly ways,
throwing food into his mouth as though
the latter were a cave without a door,
and everywhere he goes this lack of
good manners makes people take a dislike to him. He certainly ought to be
told of it ; but who is to tell him ?

If it is difficult in the home, what
must it be in the case of the high ones
of the earth, to whom all the
world turns a courtier face ?
Some time ago I was asked
to meet at luncheon a very great lady,
one whom in my thoughts I had placed
on a sort of pedestal on account of her
beauty, her high place in the world,
and her many sorrows. I was delighted,
and eagerly accepted the invitation.
The lady was beautiful still, in spite of
her grey hair, but all her charm is

Cowardice with friends.

A penalty of eminence.

spoiled by a habit of almost incessant snorting—no less vivid word will express it! At the luncheon table it was not only excessively pronounced, but additionally disagreeable. Romance had shone like a star in all my thoughts about this great lady until then, but the radiance died away on the instant and has never again returned—"*Alles ist weg!*" And such a trifle, too, after all! If only some one had dared to deal faithfully with that great lady there would be nothing to disgust or offend about her.

We know ourselves so little that we should carefully cherish an acute distrust, and be ready to suspect in our own persons the existence of some flaw or imperfection for every one we detect in others. Perhaps it is an inward consciousness that we live in a glass house that makes us fear to throw stones.

Glass houses?

It is with a quaking heart that the mistress of a household remonstrates with her maids on any point in which they have failed in duty. It needs considerable moral courage to discharge oneself of this necessary task. One puts off the evil moment as long as possible, and meditates in the night watches as to the most feasible plan of getting it done. And very often the point is weakly abandoned. We cannot risk exposing ourselves to the "tongue-thrashing" in which some of the base-

Correcting the maids.

61

ment ladies are such gifted performers. The safest way is always to mingle praise with blame, just as we hide a powder in jam. "You are always so very neat, Mary, that I am sure this cannot be neglect, but just a little bit of forgetfulness."

A recipe for fault-finding.

Or, "Your soups are generally so excellent, cook, that," &c. This is a good recipe for fault-finding, and it works well, too, with our equals, though, of course, one has to be doubly careful in dealing courteously with so sensitive a class as servants.

The fact is, we are cowards all, in face of any duty that threatens to affect the sunshiny atmosphere of home. We dread the clouds with a mortal fear, and are prone to sacrifice far more than we ought on the altar of Peace and Love. They are good and beautiful things, but they may be too dearly bought. And, above all, we must beware of indulging ourselves in them to the detriment of the best interests of others.

Cowards all!

The Duchess of Teck, with all her *bonhomie* and graciousness of manner, was one of the most dignified of women. She could administer a rebuke, too, without uttering a word. I shall never forget her look when, on a semi-public, outdoor occasion, an individual of the civic kind approached her with his hat on his head. He had taken it off on his approach, but calmly replaced it as he stood before the, Duchess and her husband. A gleam of fun shone in the Duke's eyes as he watched the episode. The Duchess, meanwhile, in dead silence, simply looked at the hat. The look was enough. Those large grey eyes of hers were eloquent. They said, as plainly as if the words had been spoken, "My good man, you are guilty of a very flagrant breach of etiquette. What a very ignorant person you must be!"

The wearer of the hat looked puzzled for a single instant as he marked the eyes of the Duchess fixed firmly on his head-gear. In another moment his hat was in his hand, and his face, ears, and neck were suffused with a most painful scarlet. He was all one abject apology. The Duchess, then, with a significant glance, quietly proceeded with the matter in hand.

A GLASS OF WINE.

I AM no advocate of total abstinence. Quite the contrary! I am sorry for the man who has to bind himself down by oaths and vows to refrain from drink, because he knows that he cannot leave off when he has had enough. But if he abstains, not from any knowledge of inward weakness, but from the same motive that urged St. Paul to say: "I would not eat meat while the world lasts, lest I make my brother to offend," then I honour him with all my heart. And this is honestly the principle on which many become total abstainers, women as well as men.

But what I want to get at is the ordinary everyday practice of drinking wine, which most of us follow in some degree or other. I do not refer to excessive drinking, inebriety, or anything of that kind, but merely the customary glass or two of wine at lunch, and two or three glasses at dinner. This can in no possible way be regarded as a bad habit. It is, in fact, the usual thing in polite society, and girls are brought up to it, and when they marry,

64

A GLASS OF WINE.

and perhaps find that among other expensive habits this one has to be given up, they miss their glass of wine rather badly at first. Why

Why should we have wine? should we have wine? That is the real question. There is no very particular reason why those who can afford it should *not* drink wine; but why should they do it? I think I could give a better set of reasons *contra* than *pro* in this matter.

First comes the one already referred to: that circumstances may not always admit of their indulging

Reasons against the habits. themselves in this rather expensive habit. Good wine costs money, and cheap wine is often highly injurious.

Another good reason for not drinking wine habitually at table is that when the health is impaired by illness or low vitality arising from any cause, the invigorating effect of good wine is quite lost, owing to the system having become accustomed to it. This prevents it from acting upon the nerves and tissues as it would do most beneficially if there were any novelty about it.

A third reason for not doing it is that for patients who have made a continual practice of wine-drinking at meals, doctors are obliged, in quite nine cases out of ten, to forbid it, especially to women. And almost always they order whiskey instead. How often one hears people say nowadays—both men and women—"My doctor

5

won't let me drink wine. He says I must have whiskey and water, *if I drink anything.*"

No doubt the doctor would generally prefer that his patients should not drink even the whiskey, but he knows very well that the habit of a lifetime is not to be overcome without an amount of resolution which is by no means always forthcoming. Sir Henry Thompson, in his admirable book, "Food and Feeding," gives it as his opinion that "the *habitual* use of wine, beer, or spirits is a dietetic error." He adds to this very straight and direct pronouncement : "In other words, the great majority of people, at any age or of either sex, will enjoy better health, both of body and mind, and will live longer, without alcoholic drinks whatever than with habitual indulgence in their use, even though such use be what is popularly understood as moderate. But I do not aver that any particular harm results from the habit of now and then enjoying a glass of really fine, pure wine, just as one may occasionally enjoy a particularly choice dish ; neither the one nor the other, perhaps, being sufficiently innocuous or digestible for frequent, much less habitual, use." And there is much more to practically the same effect. So that this eminent authority regards the habit of daily drinking wine as one that is

Sir Henry Thompson's verdict.

"A dietetic error."

likely to produce more or less injurious
results upon the body, and possibly
upon the mind as well.

And I have kept to the last another
reason, and perhaps the strongest of
any, against it. That is, the
The greatest danger. ever-present danger of learning to like wine too well, and
of falling into the awful fault of drunken-
ness. I will add no word to this argument, for the miseries, degradation, and
horrors of this kind of thing are only
too well known.

Madame Sarah Bernhardt, who is
as healthy, vigorous, and charming a
woman of her age (I won't
A telling example. mention what it is!) as it
would be possible to find,
and who has preserved in a marvellous
manner her dramatic powers, attributes
her condition of blithe well-being to
her life-long habit of abstinence from
drinking wine or alcoholic beverages of
any kind. It is not that she never
touches them. Not at all! The *Grande
Sarah* can enjoy a glass of champagne
or Burgundy as well as any one—
better, in fact, than most, since she has
never accustomed herself to their constant use. She likes milk, and if any
woman wants to keep her complexion
at its best she should take to this un-
sophisticated beverage at once and
abide by it.

There is no reason whatever that we
should not enjoy wine at dinner-parties.
I am so afraid of being misunderstood

that I must run some risk of repeating myself. It is only with the habitual daily use of wine at lunch and dinner that I am finding fault. It serves no good end. But, on occasion, let it be enjoyed like other good gifts of a kindly Providence. Because some misuse it and abuse it there is no compulsion to avoid it upon those who do neither. If every one of the moderate drinkers in England were to become teetotallers there would be just the same number of drunkards left in the land, pursuing their own courses. They would not be affected by the abstinence of others.

The habitual use only deprecated.

A dinner-party without wine is rather a mournful business. I was at one once. It was several years ago, but I have never forgotten it. It was the first occasion on which I ever tasted a frightful temperance drink called "gooseberry champagne." It is also likely to be the last! Oh, no! Do not let us have wineless dinner-parties! The very point of my argument is that if we refrain from the habit of drinking it daily our enjoyment of it on such social occasions is very greatly enhanced. But what are we to drink? I fully admit that the perfect drink has yet to be invented. Water would be good enough for most of us if we could only get it pure. But this is difficult indeed. And even if our water supply were to be immaculate we should lack

A mournful dinner-party.

faith in its perfection! Could we have
our glass jugs filled at some far-off
mountain rill, miles away from London
smoke and its infected atmosphere, we
should have to look no further for a delicious drink, pure, invigorating, and of
so simple a character as leaves the
flavours of food unimpaired for the
palate.

Sweet drinks are not recommended
as accompaniments to solid food. But
there is no lack of good
A sub-stitute. aërated waters, sparkling and
most inviting of aspect, as
well as pleasant to the palate for those
who have not spoiled it by the constant
use of wine.

Now, I wonder if any single reader
of this will give up even one glass of
wine daily, or keep her young sons
and daughters from falling into the
habit of constantly taking it at meals?
I can assure the doubtful that there is
nothing unusual in dispensing with it.
The question asked by one's host or
hostess at a restaurant: "What wine do
you like?" is often, and more especially
at luncheon, answered by: "None,
thanks; I like apollinaris, distilled
water," &c. The experiment of doing
without wine is worth trying.

SOME OLD PROVERBS.

IN an old book that is one of my treasures, having been published in the year 1737, I find much wisdom that is applicable to our conduct in every-day life. It purports to be a " Compleat Collection of English Proverbs ; also the most celebrated Proverbs of the Scotch, Italian, French, and Other Languages." Very early in the volume comes the saying that " Discreet women have neither eyes nor ears." Have we not all to practise this kind of discretion in our home dealings ? In vulgar parlance, we " wink at " much that goes on in the kitchen, and profit largely in the matter of peace and quiet by doing so. Should we hear the servants disagree, a convenient deafness seizes us ; for we know very well that if we were to inquire into the bearings of the business a slightly boisterous wind would very soon develop into a hurricane. And does not the exercise of tact in many cases compel us to shut our eyes to the traces of tears on dear faces when we know that any reference to the cause would upset

"Discreet women have neither eyes nor ears."

composure and bring with it the feeling
of humiliation that follows loss of self-
control before others. The happiest
homes are those in which " discreet
women have neither eyes nor ears,"
except when vigilance is thoroughly in
season.

From the Spanish comes the proverb,
" A great dowry is a bed full of brabbles." Was there ever an
heiress yet who did not find
it so? Who did not, at least
once in her life, long to
be rid of the riches that made life so
difficult for her, obscuring true love, and
making the parting of the ways so impossibly difficult of choice? And even
when the disinterested lover is chosen
there are many, many unhappy hours
caused by the miserable money. A man
loves his pride far more than he loves
any woman, and often sacrifices home
happiness to it. There is no lack of
" brabbles " (brambles) in any woman's
life who possesses wealth. Riches
might be supposed to be a great ease-
ment to existence, but if the poorly
endowed could but realise their im-
munity from cares of a heavy kind they
would, like the psalmist, choose "neither
riches nor poverty." Even a small
dowry serves to bring the sharks round
a girl, and she is far safer without more
than the merest competence. To have
to do some work in the world is good
for her, and many a devoted parent who
works hard to leave his girls well pro-

" A great dowry is a bed of brambles."

vided for would have done far better
for them if he had equipped them with
the means of earning their own living.
There would be fewer "brabbles" in
their path. There are thousands and
thousands of discontented women in
England now who are weighted with
their own idle and selfish lives, and
owe it all to the selfless affection of
a father who worked himself into his
grave in order to place them beyond
the reach of want.

Oh! The waste of beautiful things
in this weary world! The bootless love
that blindly strives for the welfare of
the loved ones! The endless pains and
self-denial that elicit nothing but in-
gratitude! Who has not read "Père
Goriot"? Have any of us forgotten
King Lear? Fathers, do not burden
your daughters with great dowries.
Life is hard enough on women without
adding the penalty of great riches to the
weird they have to dree.

"The best mirror is an old friend."
Most truly 'tis so. There are we safe
from flattery. We sometimes
see in our looking-glasses
rather what we wish to see
than what is really reflected.
Du Maurier had once in *Punch* a
portrait of Mrs. Somebody as she
really was, another sketch of the lady
as she appeared to herself, and a third
as her husband saw her. The husband
represented the "old friend" in this instance, and his idea of his wife was far

"The best mirror is an old friend."

72

from flattering. It is so with many husbands ; but not with all. Quite recently there was published a sonnet, written by an eminent man on seeing his wife's portrait when she was well on into middle age. The expression of surprise in discovering that any one could see an elderly woman in the wife of his youth, in whom he saw always, when he looked at her, her own young face, was exquisitely put, and the whole sonnet most touchingly conveyed the truth that some "old friends" see dear but faded faces through a glamour of affection, that equals that of even vanity itself.

"An hungry man an angry man." Well! Here is good guidance for us. *Punch's* immortal "Feed the brute!" endorses it with a note of modernity, and the far-off echo from the early days of the eighteenth century proves that human nature is not much altered in this respect. Is it not a good recommendation for punctuality with meals ? But how many men will approve of the following : "Dry bread at home is better than roast meat abroad." In these days of restaurant lunches and dinners all that kind of thing might be supposed to have altered ; but, even now, many a man prefers a chop at home to mock turtle in the city. Home food does him more good, he thinks. Is there anything in it beyond imaginings ?

"Life is half spent before we know

what it is." How often we wish we could have our time over again, and how differently we should spend it, with the light of experience to guide us!

"Life is half spent before we know what it is."

It was our tragic ignorance that misled us, we think. We had no chart to show us where the quicksands lay. We could so easily have avoided them, or so we believe. If we had only taken the other turning, we say. It was at that parting of the roads that we lost our way. There were no finger-posts for our understanding, and the experience of friends we rejected as unsuitable to our own case. And, oh! how "full of brabbles" have we found the path. We missed the smooth, broad highway, and met many an ugly fence and trudged many a weary foot in muddy lanes and across ploughed fields. If we had only known! The sweetness of the might-have-been smiles upon us from its infinite distance, far, far beyond our reach, with the light upon it that never was on land or sea. *Si jeunesse savait!* But, then, if it did, it would no longer be youth. And, after all, we were not meant to walk firmly and safely and wisely at the first trial, any more than the baby who totters and sways and balances himself, only to totter again, and suddenly collapse with the deep and solemn gravity of babyhood, under the laughing, tender eyes of the watchful mother. Are there not

"God has His plan for every man."

wise and loving eyes watching our wanderings and noting our sad mistakes? And cannot good come out of evil? Thank God, it can, and many a life that looks like failure here on earth may be one of God's successes.

Remember the good old Swiss proverb:—

> "God has His plan
> For every man."

CANDOUR AS A HOME COMMODITY.

WHY is it that members of some households consider themselves at liberty to make the rudest remarks to each other on subjects that ought to be sacred ground ? We all know the old saying which tells us that fools rush in where angels fear to tread, and when we find strangers from without the home circle inter-meddling with the bitter griefs of its members, we are full of condemnation. For instance, when a callous question was asked of a girl in mourning as to whom she was wearing it for, the indignation of those in hearing of it knew no bounds. But there are other griefs than bereavement, and sometimes they are even harder to bear. If perfect freedom of remark is habitually indulged in, the habit grows, and grows, and the operator at last becomes so hardened to the sight of the pain she inflicts that it makes no impression on her—no more than a hedgehog's prickles make on their proprietor.

The brutality of some qualities of candour.

There is far too much candour in family life ! Like all perversions of good qualities, it is more aggravating than many wholly bad ones. The possessor can always make out such a good case for herself. " I always say what I think," is one of the favourite expressions of these candid folk. "I never flatter any one," is another of their pet sayings, but I have always observed that a painfully frank person is by no means rigidly "true and just in all her dealings," as the Catechism puts it. Quite the contrary, in fact. Such persons seem to use up all their stock of candour in dealing round heart-aches and planting roots of bitterness wherever they find an opportunity. They have none left for occasions when it is obviously against their own interests to be very honest and open. Double-dealing often lurks behind an exaggerated appearance of frankness.

The painfully frank person not always a model of justice.

The cultivation of politeness in the home averts much of this element of *brusquerie* and unnecessary candour with their consequences of ill-will and wounded spirits. Politeness need not mean stiffness, as some folk seem to fancy that it does. It is only when it is but occasionally donned and not habitually worn that it becomes inseparable from a feeling of *gêne*. "Company manners" should not be very different from those of everyday life, but those of every day are often lamentably insufficient.

Politeness need not mean stiffness.

77

The reason that so many wounds can be dealt to those at home by the wielders of the weapon of candour is "A prophet is not honoured." that we are known with all our faults to the members of the home circle. Our weaknesses cannot expect to escape the notice of those who see us every day, and it is only after long practice that we learn to receive the thrusts of the overcandid with a patient forbearance. Sometimes we are fain to acknowledge that we have profited by the sound and wholesome home-truths conveyed to us by their means, but it needs a noble nature to accept in this way The alchemy of noble natures. what was meant as a daggerthrust. There are cases where some natural defect is made the butt of sneers and rude remarks, as when a sister remarks to a brother, " Pity you're so short, Jack !" when she knows very well that poor Jack would willingly give a finger to be the length of it taller. These nasty little jests are not forgotten, and when the day comes that the sister might exert a beneficent influence over Jack, she finds that he is armed against her by the memory of her own words.

A very hateful form of candour is that which impels people to reveal family secrets, which have for some Revealing family secrets. very good reason been kept from some of the members. "They think it only right that he should know," and straightway proceed to inform him, whoever he may be, without even giving the unfortunate relatives the chance of telling him themselves. Such a case occurred once in a family with which I had some acquaintance. A woman, who was not even a relative, revealed a carefully-guarded secret to a boy who was still too young to realise the importance of keeping it to himself. Consequently it soon became public property, and when, after an interval, the truth was discovered as to how the boy came to know the facts, the person who had told him was heard to express surprise that she was never invited to the So-and-so's now! It would have been more surprising if she had been! There are officious people of this sort to be found in every circle, and it is always safer to keep them at a distance. Two such are enough to set a whole city by the ears.

Candour is a delightful and a refreshing quality; of that there can be not the smallest doubt. And cold *Candour and cold water.* water is refreshing! It is nice to have a little drink or a pleasant bath, but no one likes his head held under the pump, for all that! Nor do we enjoy being forced to drink cold water when we are not thirsty, do we? But that is analogous to what the over-candid people make us *That delightful word "Tact"!* do. Hypocrisy is hateful enough, but we all know it for what it is, and sometimes a small dose of it is really preferable to a draught of candour, administered without compunction, the operator holding the nose of the victim, as it were.

It is, at least, not a commodity to be laid in in large quantities, is it ? And even when we feel very well supplied, we need not be lavish with it. No one will be much poorer if we keep our stores untouched, and we ourselves shall certainly be richer. For does not unnecessary outspokenness rob us of the affection and sympathy of those without whom the world would be an empty and a dreary place ? We want all the love we can get to help us through the world, and when we favour others with a burst of candour we sadly diminish our share of goodwill. It is like the *peau de chagrin* in Balzac's famous story, which contracted whenever the owner used up any of the joys of life, and when it shrank into nothingness he had to die. So it is with our unkind speeches. They lose us the only life worth living, that which is in the thoughts and affections of our friends. And it is extraordinary how long they are remembered. They stick like burrs long after the pleasant, kindly words of praise and appreciation are forgotten.

"To be administered in small doses."

La peau de chagrin.

GOLDEN SILENCE.

" What did the Colonel's lady think ?
　　Nobody never knew.
Somebody asked the Sergeant's wife,
　　An' she told 'em true !
When you get to a man in the case,
　　They're like as a row of pins,
For the Colonel's lady an' Judy O'Grady
　　Are sisters under their skins ! "

RUDYARD KIPLING.

"UNDER their skins." Perhaps. But note the reticence of the Colonel's lady.

The reticence of the Colonel's lady. " Nobody never knew " what she thought about it all, and what would the world be if the typical gentlewoman did not exercise self-control ? If every woman were to be as outspoken as Judy O'Grady, society would rapidly fall to pieces. The lesson of quiet composure has to be learned soon or late, and it is generally soon in the higher classes of society. In fact the quality of reticence, and even stoicism, is so early implanted in the daughters of the cultivated classes that a rather trying monotony is sometimes the result. After a while the girls outgrow it, learning how to exercise the acquired habit of self-control without losing the charm of individuality. When maturity is reached, one of the most **A delightful social quality.** useful and delightful of social qualities is sometimes attained —not always—that of silently passing over much that, if noticed, would make for discord. Truth to tell, there is often far too much talking going on. A little incident **Unintentional slights.** occurs over which some one feels slighted or offended. Perhaps the slight or offence was most unintentional, but as we all know, there are many "sensitive" women who are ever ready to make a molehill into a mountain. This is the moment for a judicious and golden silence. The wise woman will not imitate Judy O'Grady and make her moan to every one she meets about the rudeness of that ill-bred Mrs. So-and-so. This is the very best means of magnifying the affair. Let it rest. An explanation is sure, or almost sure, to be given, but if, in the meanwhile, any quantity of talk has been going on, the explanation which was perfectly adequate to the original occasion, seems remarkably incomplete and lacking in spontaneity.

Suppose that an omission has been made of some particular acquaintance in sending out invitations to a ball. The lady who is left out in the cold, unless she happens to be one of the "sensitive" contingent, immediately comes to the conclusion that there is a mistake somewhere, that a note has been lost in the post, or delivered at the wrong address, or something of that kind. She keeps quiet about it, saying no unnecessary word on the subject, except, perhaps, to a very intimate friend of her own, who also knows the giver of the ball well, and who may be able to throw some light on the matter. The chances are that the mistake will be cleared up. But the "sensitive" beings whose feelings are always "trailing their coats," like the stage Irishman, make such a hubbub and to-do that they render it difficult for the hostess of the occasion to remedy any oversight that may have been made, without the appearance of having been forced into it.

How the "Colonel's lady" would treat the matter.

Sometimes a whole "snowball" of scandal is collected by some one starting the merest flake, so to speak. "I wonder if Mrs. Such-an-one is all right," is quite enough to set the matter going. The person to whom this remark has been made says to some one else, "Lady Blank thinks Mrs. Such-an-one is a bad lot," and still more colour is given to the next remark, so that the simile of the snowball justifies itself. Is not this a case when silence proves itself to be golden indeed? And not only in the interests of charity is this so, but sometimes for reasons of pure policy as well. A lady who had permitted her expres-

"The Sergeant's wife."

sions about a certain person of her acquaintance to pass the bounds of discretion was, a few seasons since, called to account by the husband of the libelled individual, and a most unpleasant scene ensued. It was quite right that she should have had to undergo some unpleasantness, for she had made at least one woman most undeservedly miserable, and had almost caused a separation between her and her husband. Had this really resulted no one would have believed in the innocence of the unfortunate wife. A complete recantation and full apology followed, and the perpetrator of the scandal disappeared for many months from amid her circle of acquaintances.

And is not silence golden in the home? If there is even one member who is kindly and charitable, and who makes allowances for small failings, looking for the good in everybody and taking a lenient view of other people's shortcomings, the effect is surprising. The little leaven leaveneth the whole lump in time, and the "soft answer" becomes the fashion of the household. "Hcw very rude Edith was this morning at the breakfast table!" says some one, feeling aggrieved by the harshness of some rebuke administered by one who had neither right nor reason to find fault. If the interlocutor replies, "Yes, shameful ; I wouldn't stand it ; I should tell her of it, if I were you," then the

The little leaven in the home.

84

flame is fanned, and may result in a general conflagration, in which friendliness, goodwill, and serenity are consumed to ashes. But if a discreet silence on all aggravating cir-

Blessed are the peacemakers. cumstances is observed the affair may blow over very quietly. Suppose that some such reply as the following is made : " Oh, well, you know what Edith is. She is easily put out, and she had just had a very annoying letter. You may be sure she is very sorry by this time for the way she spoke to you." At once the calming effect of gentleness and reticence is felt, and when the belligerents next meet it is only to find that peace is concluded, war at an end.

Blessed are the peacemakers !

A perfectly frightful amount of talking goes on in some families. Each

Family amenities. member is picked to pieces, as it were, motives found for her conduct that would astonish her indeed if she heard them attributed to her, and her kindest and most disinterested actions are distorted to suit the narrow minds and selfish ideas of those who are discussing her. Incapable of magnanimity themselves, such people translate kindheartedness and single-mindedness by the dim little light that is within their own petty minds, and the result is just what might be expected from the process. Light becomes darkness, purity foulness, goodness evil. There are women—not

at all the worst in the world, but
a silly, selfish, empty-headed class of
unconscious mischief-makers — who,
when they talk together, produce a
kind of brew like that of the Witches
in " Macbeth."

> " Fillet of a fenny snake
> In the cauldron boil and bake ;
> Eye of newt, and toe of frog,
> Wool of bat, and tongue of dog,
> Lizard's leg, and owlet's wing,
> Adder's fork, and blindworm's sting,
> For a charm of powerful trouble
> Let the hell-broth boil and bubble."

Many a little fault, deeply repented,
would pass and be forgotten, except in
the sorrowing penitence of
the faulty one, if only a
stream of talk had not flowed
around and about it, bitter as
the waters of Marah. Often and often
when friends look coldly on each other,
each wondering why the other should
seem estranged, the cause may be
found to lie in a " long talk," in which
some one has indulged, with the result
that actions are misrepresented, hasty
words exaggerated, and charged with
meaning they were never meant to carry,
and remarks repeated in a manner that
gives them an unkind bearing they
were never intended to convey. " I
wonder why Mary did not stop for a
word or two, as she always does when
we meet ? She looked rather stiff, I
thought." "Oh, I suppose . . . . has

The confidential whisperers.

86

been talking to her and making mischief. You know what she is!"

Yes; that's how it's done. It is only what might be expected from poor Judy O'Grady; but the Colonel's lady is not always above the level of the "whisperer" who "separates chief friends."

I say again—

"Blessed are the peacemakers."

A SOCIAL CONSCIENCE.

CONSCIENCES can be cultivated, like voices, and it would do the world no harm if there were professors who would give courses of lessons on their cultivation.

Conscience classes.

The young woman whose hat-pin pierced the eye of a young man who was unfortunate enough to sit next to her on the top of a Liverpool omnibus stood in need of a few lessons. If hat-pins are a necessity—and I admit that they are —it should also be necessary to exercise care in their disposition. It is quite possible to render them effectual and yet harmless by pushing them slightly back after having thrust them through the crown of the hat. And any one in whom a social conscience is properly developed will see to it that her hat-pins are not unnecessarily long. For instance, a six-inch hat crown cannot possibly require a ten-inch pin. It is terrible to see the armoury of sharp-pointed pins that jut out at the sides of some women's heads.

The hat-pin terror.

Another point in which the members

of our sex show a total absence of social conscience is the manner in which they carry a sunshade or umbrella. The latter is often, when open, held down over the head of a rather short woman in a way that is certainly protective of herself and her headgear, but which is extremely inconvenient, and sometimes even dangerous, to those who share the footpath or pavement with her. The points of her umbrella catch in the hair or dress, and sometimes threaten the eyes of passers-by.

Umbrellas as weapons of offence.

When closed, the sunshade or umbrella often becomes equally a weapon of offence, being carried in the arms with the knob or crook of the handle protruding. A smart blow is often administered to the unwary passer in this way, and among the dangers of the streets, numerous enough without, may now be catalogued the shouldered sunshade of our sex.

It is not often that we imitate the equally dangerous method in which some men carry sticks and umbrellas, viz., under the arm, with the ferule protruding at the back, a danger to the eyes of those behind ; nor do we, as a rule, prod the pavement with our parasols, as so many men do with their sticks or umbrellas, letting them drag after them, so that those who come behind are apt to fall over them. But, on the other hand, our husbands are

Male injustices.

A SOCIAL CONSCIENCE.

free from the offence of opening sun-
shades in a crowd, with an upward
scrape of all the points.

And then there is the matinée hat!
Oh, sisters, where is the social conscience of those among us
who of malice aforethought
attend the theatre with all-
impeding and obstructive
headgear? A knowledge of the senti-
ments we excite in the bosoms of those
behind us might help some of us to be
a little unselfish in the matter. Posi-
tive, if temporary, detestation is the
principal emotion entertained towards
the wearer of a matinée hat, and the
hatred is not unmingled with con-
tempt; for who can help despising a
girl or woman who is openly and
avowedly careless of the inconvenience
and disappointment she is causing?
Man's ideal of woman depicts her as
so exactly the opposite of this that he
cannot fail to resent the disillusion.

Of all the forms of social lack of
conscience, one of the most irritating
is the way some women have
of making calls on the off
days, other than those on
which the callee announces
herself to be "at home." Especially
is this annoying if the person called on
happens to be a busy woman. She has
probably arranged her "day" in self-
defence from intrusion on all others,
but to do so is no safeguard against
the unconscionable acquaintance who

The matinée hat.

Calls on wrong days.

90

A SOCIAL CONSCIENCE.

prefers to suit her own convenience rather than that of her friends. And if sometimes she comes in in very wet garments and flounces down on one's velvet-covered couch, why, she may be described as adding injury to insult.

It is really almost insulting to call on an off day, for it means either that one's caller hopes to find one absent or else that she intends to monopolise one's attention after having flagrantly disregarded one's wishes.

There are fine opportunities for the display of "no conscience" in travelling. It is so pleasant, for
Travelling sans conscience. instance, to share a railway carriage with a person who insists on keeping the windows closed. And, without going into detail, I may refer to travellers by sea who make an inferno of the ladies' cabin, when the weather is rough, simply for lack of consideration for others.

There are minor ways in which this form of thoughtlessness may be displayed. In doing up postal
Some minor failings. packets one may consider the postman, and refrain from tying up half a dozen newspapers in one bundle just for the sake of saving oneself the trouble of writing the address three or four times. In an omnibus it is unnecessary to point the stick of one's umbrella outwards, so that every one who enters is in danger of falling over it. Yet many women do

this. There are those, too, who lounge
sideways in a crowded omnibus, while
their neighbours are screwed up un-
comfortably closely for lack of the
inches that should be theirs, but which
the lounger has appropriated.

And who shall say that conscience is
perfectly developed in the woman who
keeps her coachman and foot-
man waiting for hours in the
cold of a winter's night while
she is warmly housed and indifferent ?
Or in her whose maid has to sit up for
her till the small hours, and yet has to
fetch her her cup of tea bright and early
the next morning ? And what shall be
said of her who goes to her dressmaker
and orders a gown at the very last
moment ? Where is her social conscience ? Does she not know that
weary girls who have worked hard all
day must be kept late to complete her
dress ? Does she know ? Does she
care ? And what of her who omits to
pay her milliner, her dressmaker, her florist, and all
others who supply her with
the luxuries of life ? Her conscience
must be of the most diminutive order.
In things great and small the lack of
social conscience shows itself. As compared with a few particulars I have
mentioned, the want of punctuality is a trifle, but it is
sometimes productive of the
most aggravating effects. And
there are women who almost appear

Those poor servants!

And trades-people!

The unpunctual woman.

to take pains to be unpunctual, so invariably are they just too late for everything. What they cost their housemates in time and temper can never be computed. They are themselves serene. "I'm the most unpunctual of human beings," one such will be heard to say. She keeps people fuming on a platform watching train after train start for Henley, Ascot, Sandown, or Hurlingham, and comes up smiling and saying, "I'm afraid all you dear people are very cross with me." At mealtimes she is equally exasperating, but she never seems to be aware that her consistent unpunctuality makes her a terrible trial to all her acquaintances. She is destitute of social conscience. And I might cite a hundred other instances of this destitution were it necessary !

OUR DEBTS.

IT would be a lovely world if there were
no credit system. Think of the mill-
stones some of us hang round
our necks in the shape of
debts, all on account of this
temptation. In one of Mr.
Howell's books, he makes the father
of a family say to his children :
" Don't spend money if you haven't got
any." The advice seems superfluous,
and would be so if we had to pay
ready money for everything we buy.
But it is, in existing circumstances, only
too easy to spend money that we have
not got ; from the dealings in the Stock
Exchange down to the fishmonger's
round the corner.

There are two ways of looking at the
matter—one from the purchaser's point
of view, the other from the
seller's. I intend to take
the purchaser's first, having
long thought the credit system highly
demoralising to many who might have
thriven and prospered bravely had
not its insinuating temptations been
thrown in their way. It is so fatally

"If there
were no
credit
system!"

Two points
of view.

94

easy to order a quantity of nice things,
to be paid for in a nebulous
"Facilis est descensus." future, which always seem a
long way off. And then,
when the grip of it all begins to be felt,
we are afraid *not* to go on ordering, lest
our creditor should be offended and
dun us for his " little account." And so
we get deeper and deeper in debt, and
soon begin to lose our footing in the
financial whirlpool. Oh, the misery of
it ! The long, sleepless nights of worry
and despair, the irritable frame of mind
thereby engendered, the loss of self-
respect, the inability to make the most
of our income while in debt, and the
consequent hopelessness of ever extri-
cating ourselves — all, all might be
avoided if we were forced to pay on
the spot for every purchase.

That the credit system has its advan-
tages is more than possible ; but I am
not looking for them just at this
moment. I want to sketch a gloomy
picture, with the hope of inducing all
who look upon it to abandon the habit
of running long accounts, with its often
ruinous results. The inexperienced
young wife, unaccustomed to
The young wife's initial error. deal with large sums of
money, often cripples her
hard - working husband by
falling most unconsciously into the
snares of the system as it exists. In
her desire to have everything comfortable, inviting, and agreeable for
him in the home in his hours of

leisure, she launches out in "ordering" all that she thinks would aid her in this unquestionably excellent object. Money always promises to do a great deal more than it ever actually accomplishes. It is one of its most *An odious characteristic.* odious characteristics, and the novice never dreams but that the incoming sums will cover all her outlay. Then comes the tug-of-war, and if she has no moral courage she struggles on without laying the whole matter before her husband, and is soon in a network of difficulties. He has to know, soon or late, and the resultant rift within the lute is by no means little. It is a very bad start! And when the wife would like to dress her little ones daintily and prettily, she finds herself unable to spend upon them anything beyond what may pay for absolute necessaries. If her punishment had not begun before, it very certainly commences then.

And is not the poor husband to be pitied? He had, no doubt, the idea that all women, after their *The poor husband.* schooldays, are apt housewives, and entrusted to his young wife the entire management of the household. It is hard on him when he finds that all is chaos in the exchequer, and that he has to deny himself for years in many ways in order to pay debts that should never have been contracted.

Think of the delightful difference

there might have been in the little
family were there no such
If "trust" thing as "trust" in trade,
were not. the children beautifully
dressed and the pride of a happy
mother; the father in good humour
and gaiety of heart, enjoying his home
as a man ought, who works to maintain it ; and the sunshine of prosperity
pervading every room of it !

Thousands and thousands of homes
have been ruined by the credit system.
The only means of averting such disaster is the exercise of strength of mind
in resisting the temptation. This involves a splendid, but extremely costly,
education in moral fortitude, to those
who possess but little of such strength
and have to acquire it by long and sad
experience.

It might help some to resist running
long accounts if they were to realise
that doing so is really borrow-
The mean- ing money from their trades-
ness of it.
people. Yes, madam ! That
£5 you owe your laundress is just so
much borrowed of the poor woman,
and without interest, too. And can you
bear to think of the anxiety of mind it
costs her, poor, hard-working creature ;
for how can she tell that you will ever
pay her ? There is your dressmaker,
too. How much have you compulsorily
borrowed of her ? You owe her £100,
perhaps. And for how long has it been
owing ? You pay £10 or so off it, and
order another gown ; and so it has

been going on for years and years.
You don't see why you should have
to pay your dressmaker money down
when your husband never thinks of
paying his tailor under three or four
years.

Well, two wrongs never yet made a
right, and the fact that men of fashion
never pay their tailors until
"Two wrongs." they have been dunned over
and over again for the money
is only another item in the indictment
against the credit system.

It is undignified to owe money to any
one, and more particularly to one's
social inferiors, but this view of the
subject is too seldom taken. Can any
one dispute it, however? We badly
want it to be made plain to the eyes of
the whole community.

One disagreeable result of the credit
system is the raising of the market price
of commodities in order to
Increased cover the losses resultant to
prices. the trader. Not only do bad
debts occur, which have to be written
off the books, but being "out of one's
money" for years means loss of interest.
Those who pay ready money are sometimes, and should always be, allowed discount off all payments, but even when
this is done it does not suffice to meet the
claims of absolute justice in the matter,
the scales of prices having been adjusted
to cover losses owing to the credit
system.

Tradesmen have to charge high rates

or they could not keep on their business, and the hard part of it

The sufferers. is that the very persons who enable them to keep going by paying their accounts weekly are those who suffer most from the system, paying a fifth or so more than they need were all transactions "money down."

And now for the other side of the question. It has often been said that tradesmen like customers to

The other side. run long accounts. Let any one who believes this buy a few of the trade papers, and see what they have to say on the subject. Let them visit a few of the West End Court milliners and ask them what their opinion of the matter is. Let them interview the managers of large drapery houses. They will soon find that the tradesman has a distinct grievance in the credit system. Here is what one dressmaker says, and she is only one of a very numerous class, every member of which is in exactly similar circumstances.

She is a clever and enterprising woman who had opened an establishment for the sale of all kinds

A dressmaker's opinion. of articles for ladies' wear, and complains bitterly that, though she is doing a good trade, all her money has become "buried in her books." She is making money with her extending business, "but," she says, "I really have less command of cash than at any time in my life. The fact is my

savings are all lent to rich people."
Asked for an example, she said : "The
last bill I receipted this morning will
do. Ten months ago a lady

A case in point. came into the shop, talked
pleasantly on Church matters,
in which I am interested, bought nearly
£30 worth of goods, after very sharp
bargaining, that reduced my profits to
the narrowest margin, and went away.
To have suggested payment during
these ten months would have been
regarded as an insult, and I should have
lost her custom for ever. I have often
been in need of the money. She is the
wife of a very high ecclesiastical digni-
tary, is regarded as philanthropic, talks
about self-help among women, and very
likely visited my shop in that spirit ;
yet though she is undoubtedly rich she
borrowed £30 of my capital for ten
months without paying any interest."

"If I could only get a little money in
from my customers," said a hard-worked

A second opinion. West End milliner to me one
day during a very hot and
exhausting May, "I could run
off to the seaside or to Scotland for a
week, and take my poor old mother,
who needs a change even more than I do.
But I can't get any of my ladies to pay."
"Write and tell them how it is," I
suggested. "Oh, no! That would
never do," was the reply. "I should
offend them terribly, and they would
not only never come back themselves,
but would pass the word round among

their friends that I am given to
dunning."

One of these ladies owed her £800,
and probably still owes some of it,
though that was three or four seasons
since ; for her way of paying off is to
order a thirty-guinea gown or two,
and pay in £50 or £100 to her credit.
The truth is that the system is chiefly
responsible for the enormous
One result
of the
system.
cost of fashionable dress
nowadays, since the only
means the purveyors can
adopt to secure themselves against loss
is to charge exorbitant prices. When
their customers practically borrow all
their money of them, they are well
justified in charging interest on it in
some form or other. This naturally
results in raising the market value of
well - cut and skilfully - constructed
dresses, &c., and bears very hardly on
those who pay their way with ready-
money.

Would it not be an excellent idea to
form a society of women in aristocratic
circles who would bind them-
A "ready-
money"
association.
selves to pay ready-money for
all articles purchased ? They
could demand, and would
certainly obtain, a substantial discount
on all such payments, and with the thin
edge of the wedge thus inserted the
reform would soon be well on its way
to permanent establishment.

THE DOMESTIC GIRL.

Do not for a moment imagine that the domestic girl cannot be smart. She can turn herself out as bewitchingly as anybody, and the same cleverness that goes into her delicious *entrées*, capital sauces, and truly lovely afternoon tea-cakes concerns itself with the ripples of her coiffure, the correct tilt of her hat, and the deft fall of her skirt. The domestic girl need be neither plain nor dowdy. Plenty of exercise and the feeling that she is of use in the world brighten her eyes, keep her complexion clear, and give her that air of lightheartedness that should, but does not always, characterise a girl. How middle-aged is the expression that some of them wear! Both boys and girls in their early twenties have occasionally this elderly look.

Of course there is always the extreme domestic girl, who has not a soul above puddings, whose fingers show generally a trace of flour, and whose favourite light reading is recipes. She has been sketched for us pleasantly :—

"She isn't versed in Latin, she doesn't paint on
    satin,
  She doesn't understand the artful witchery of
    eyes ;
But, oh ! sure, 'tis true and certain she is very
    pat and pert in
  Arranging the component parts of luscious
    pumpkin pies.

She cannot solve or twist 'em, viz., the plane-
    tary system ;
  She cannot tell a Venus from a Saturn in the
    skies ;
But you ought to see her grapple with the fruit
    that's known as apple,
  And arrive at quick conclusions when she
    tackles toothsome pies.

She could not write a sonnet, and she couldn't
    trim a bonnet,
  She isn't very bookish in her letter of replies ;
But she's much at home—oh, very—when she
    takes the juicy berry
  And manipulates quite skilfully symposia in
    pies."

She is well appreciated at meal-times,
that girl, but she is not the liveliest of
companions. Like the German girl,
who is trained to housewifery and little
else from her earliest years, she has a
dough-like heaviness about her when
other topics are started. But why
should she ever be domestic only ?
—and with all the world before her
whence to choose delightsome studies
and pursuits.

Then there is the girl at the other
The Blue   end of the scale. Here is
Stocking.   her portrait :—

THE DOMESTIC GIRL.

" She can talk on evolution ;
  She can proffer a solution
For each problem that besets the modern brain.
  She can punish old Beethoven,
  Or she dallies with De Koven,
Till the neighbours file petitions and complain.

  She can paint a crimson cowboy,
  Or a purple madder ploughboy
That you do not comprehend, but must admire.
  And in exercise athletic
  It is really quite pathetic
To behold the young men round her droop
    and tire.

  She is up in mathematics,
  Engineering, hydrostatics,
In debate with her for quarter you will beg.
  She has every trait that's charming,
  With an intellect alarming ;
  Yet she cannot, oh, she cannot, fry an egg !"

And let no maiden think that to
be domestic is a *bourgeois* characteristic.
Far from it. It is the
daughters of the moneyed
bourgeoisie who are the idlest
and most empty - minded.
They think it smart to be able to do
nothing. How little they know about it !
Were not our Queen's daughters taught
to cook and sew, and make themselves
useful ? Did not the Princesses of
Wales learn scientific dress-cutting?
And was not a Royal Princess, not very
long ago, initiated into the mysteries of
hair-dressing ? There is no better
judge of needlework in the kingdom
than Princess Christian. Many of the
designs used in the Royal School of

Royal cooks and millinors.

Art Needlework are from the clever pencil of Princess Louise, Marchioness of Lorne. Princess Alice, mother of the present Empress of Russia, used to cut out her children's clothes and trim their hats in the far-back days when she was Grand Duchess of Hesse, and was surrounded by the little ones. Princess Henry of Battenberg is a skilful embroidress, besides being an artist and musician. Domesticity has not proved a bar to culture in the case of any of these highly-placed women. The Empress Frederick of Germany, our Princess Royal, is one of the most intellectual and cultivated women in the world, but she is also an adept in the domestic arts. She is a sculptress, and can cleverly wield the brush, as well as her sister, the Marchioness of Lorne. So here is a shining example in high places.

And if we take a step down to Duchesses, Marchionesses, &c., we shall find that blue blood is usually associated with a taste for true British domesticity. The Duchess of Abercorn can sew beautifully. The Duchess of Sutherland can cook and make a gown. She often designs her own dresses. The Marchioness of Londonderry, one of our most famous beauties, is a utilitarian of the first water. She is one of the first authorities on lace, is a philanthropist to her pretty finger-tips, and has often taught the wives of her husband's miners how to cook the family dinner, besides instructing them in the much neglected laws of hygiene. I might multiply examples, but these might surely suffice to show that domesticity is far from being *bourgeois* and by no means incompatible with ineffable smartness.

The aristocracy of wealth imitates that of birth in such matters ; but, in order to do so, it has to be at least a generation old in riches. The *nouveaux riches* have quite other notions, and think it far beneath the dignity of their daughters to know any-

Sensible millionaires. thing about the domestic arts. But a well - known family of millionaires, which has enjoyed the companionship of our best society for fifty or sixty years, shares its idiosyncrasies on the subject of useful education for its girls. Every one of them has been brought up as if she were obliged to earn her own living. It is left to the purse-proud and the vulgar to bring up their daughters as " fine ladies." It is a grand mistake, in more ways than one, for idle people are never happy people.

The ideal girl is she who combines with high culture a love of the do-

The ideal girl. mestic and a desire to please. This last should not be so excessive as to degenerate into vanity and conceit, but should be sufficiently powerful to induce its possessor to dress attractively, keep her pretty hair at its glossiest, and be as smart and neat and up-to-date in all matters pertaining to the toilette as any of her less-useful sisters ; besides cultivating those social graces that do so much to brighten life and sweeten it by making smooth the rough ways and rendering home intercourse as agreeable and pleasant as it should be. There are girls who keep all their prettinesses for the outside world, and are anything but attractive within the home. They are by no means the ideal girls.

THE GIRL-BACHELOR.

THE girl-bachelor is often a comfortable creature. She can make a home out of the most unpromis-

A clever
nest builder. ing materials. A dreary little flat, consisting of three tiny rooms, with hardly any chance of sunshine getting into any of them for more than three minutes in the afternoon, has been known to be metamorphosed into a most inviting little nest by the exercise of taste and skill, and at a minimum of cost. Two rooms on the second floor of a dull house in a bleak street have often been transformed, by the same means, into a cheery dwelling-place. Much merry contriving goes to this result and serves to make, like quotations and patchwork, " our poverty our pride," and, indeed, there is a keen pleasure in the cutting of our coat according to our cloth ; in making ends meet with just a little pulling, and in devising ways and means of adjusting our expenditure to the very limited contents of our exchequer.

What a mistake it is to fall into an

abyss of discontent just because we are poor! Poverty may become the cause of a thousand unsuspected joys; as it certainly is an education in ever so many ways. Some of us would hardly know ourselves if we never had been poor. Did not poverty teach us to cook, to sew, to make our dresses, to trim our hats, to cover our chairs, to drape our windows, to use a dust-pan and brush and to find out at first hand the charms of active cleanliness, that may be evoked with the aid of a humble duster? And was it not poverty that taught us to appreciate the day of little things, to enjoy the scores of small pleasures that, like wild flowers, are too often passed carelessly over? It has its hardships, truly, and some of them are bitter enough, but many who now are rich enough look back to the days of " puirtith cauld," and recognise how good it was and how much it brought out of undivined capacity; yes, and looking back, can remember the actual pleasures of poverty!

" Sweet are the uses of adversity."

Is there not a pleasure in conquering circumstances—in fighting poverty and making it yield to economy, contrivance, and industry? The fight is often hard and long-continued; and there are sad cases in which it ends in failure and disaster. But when courage and endurance have resulted in victory, and firm footing has been won on the steep

The retrospect.

hill of success, it is not unpleasant to look back and scan the long years of struggle, endeavouring to compute what they have done for us ; how they have enriched, like the snows of winter, ground that might otherwise have remained for ever arid and unprofitable.

There is a wonderful cheap world to be found in London, like an *entresol* between a palatial shop and a magnificent first floor. Into this curious world the girl-bachelor soon finds her way. She knows exactly the twopenny-halfpenny little shop where she can get art-muslin at a penny-three-farthings a yard. Most of it is hideous, but she is clever at picking out the few pretty pieces. She sometimes purchases a quite beautiful bit of colour for the brightening of her rooms in the shape of pottery vases for a couple of pence. No one better than the girl-bachelor knows that the best value for her money is to be found at the little grocer's shop in a poor neighbourhood. The poor are, naturally, intent on getting at least a shillingsworth for every shilling they lay out, and no tradesman can make a living in such localities unless he purveys the best provisions at fair prices. It is notorious that customers who buy in small quantities, as the poor are obliged to do, living from hand to mouth with their few shillings a week, are more

Bargain hunting.

"The little grocer's shop."

profitable than those who can afford to buy largely, and the tradesman who conscientiously provides good wares at a moderate profit flourishes comfortably in such circumstances. Here the girl-bachelor gets her stores. Not for her are the plate-glass windows of the great West End " establishments," which have to pay high rentals and the cost of horses and carts and extra men to send round daily for the convenience of their customers. The little shop in the back street is good enough for her.

And how expert does she become in her marketing ! Such a thing as waste Her thrift. is absolutely unknown in the tiny sphere of home of which she is the centre and the sun. The bones from her miniature joints of beef and mutton are not cast away until they are white and smooth from boiling and reboiling, the stock they yield being skilfully made up into tempting soups and savoury dishes of macaroni. There is splendid training for the future house-wife in all this ; not only in A splendid training. the matter of food itself, but in the diligent industry needed to combine its preparation with the day's work, and the practical knowledge of what such work of preparation involves. The kindest and most considerate mistresses are those who know exactly how much time and trouble it takes to produce certain results.

Contrast the girl-bachelor with her

peer of the helpless sex. Look at the dingy lodging-house break-fast-table of the poor clerk.

Unfortunate man.

Do you see the crushed and soiled tablecloth, the cup and saucer rather wiped than washed, the fork with suspicious lack of clear outline along its prongs, hatefully reminiscent of previous meals, the knife powdered with brown from recent contact with the knifeboard, and the food itself untempting to the palate and not very nutritious to the system.

Cooking comes almost by nature to the bachelor-girl. With a good stove-lamp, a frying-pan, a chafing-dish, and a boilerette, with a saucepan or two and a kettle, she has an all-sufficing *batterie de cuisine*.

"Cooking comes by nature."

The wonders she can work with these are known to many of her friends, and even those with comfortable establishments of their own are often fain to confess that her cookery invites them as the achievements of the queen of their kitchen often fail to do.

And in many other essentials the girl-bachelor has the advantage of the ordinary young man. Hear what a contemporary has to say :—"The average youth, from the time he leaves school, wants unlimited tobacco for his pipes and cigarettes, and often runs to several cigars a day ; he seldom passes many hours without a glass of something — wine, spirits, or beer,

"How it strikes a contemporary."

according to his tastes or company, and he wants a good deal of amusement of the sing-song or cheap music-hall kind, to say nothing of much more expensive meals. Tobacco would not cost him much if he were content with a little smoke when the day's work was over, instead of indulging in perpetual cigarettes. The girl has none of these expenses ; she often economises, and gives herself healthy exercise by walking at least part of the way to her occupation in fine weather ; she does not smoke ; she rarely eats or drinks between meals, though she may nibble a bit of chocolate, which, after all, is wholesome food ; her mid-day meal seldom costs more than sixpence, and she is glad after working hours to get home, where she enjoys the welcome change of reading a book and making and mending her clothes, concocting a new hat, and so forth."

It is a healthy, happy, often a merry, cheery life ; and if the girl-bachelor often sighs to be rich, the wish is not allowed to generate discontent, but serves to arouse a wholesome ambition which may lead, in time, to the realisation of the wish. And who so happy, then, as the matured and cultured woman who reaps where she has sown, and finds, in the fullest development of her faculties the real meaning of the highest happiness, viz., living upward and outward to the whole height and breadth and depth of her innate possibilities.

8

THE MIDDLE-AGED CHAPERON.

MANY are the miseries of the middle-aged chaperon ! Is it not enough, think you, to see one's lost youth reflected in the blithesome scene, to remember the waltzes of long ago, to recall the partners of the past, and the pleasant homage no longer forthcoming, and to feel within a response to the music and the rhythm of the dance, ridiculously incongruous with an elderly exterior, without suffering any added woes ? And yet they are manifold. There are the draughts ! Windows opened for the relief of heated dancers, pour down cold airs on the uncovered shoulders of chilly chaperons. What cared they for draughts in the long-ago, when all the world was young ? But now a draught is a fearsome thing. But worse, far worse, is the girl who cannot dance, who treads on her partners' toes, and knocks against their knees, and is returned with a scowl to her wretched chaperon. "I know you are going to the Mumpshire ball,"

The miseries of the chaperon.

Draughts.

says some one. "Would you mind taking my girl with you?" If
The charge who cannot dance. she is a bad performer she is returned with astonishing alacrity and punctuality at the end of each dance; and quite perceptibly to her temporary guardian's practised eye is the word passed round among the young men to avoid her as they would the—something. After a few dances, a sense of vicarious guilt seizes upon the chaperon. She knows the shortcomings of her charge are to be visited partly upon herself, and she anticipates the angry glare with which each man returns the young woman, and retreats in haste, malevolently eyeing the chaperon.

And the reward? The reward is to be treated with great stiffness by the
The reward. girl's mother, and to hear that she said: "I shall never ask Mrs. What's-her-name to take my girl to a ball again. Her own daughters danced every dance, while my poor child was left out in the cold. I think they might have introduced their partners to her."

Such are the small gnat-like stings of the present moment, while the poor
Romance. chaperon is remembering the dances of long ago, the dark-eyed partner who waltzed so exquisitely, and whose grave is in the dismal African swamp so far away; the lively, laughing, joking boy who would put his name down for half a dozen dances,

only to have it promptly scratched out
again with many scoldings.   He is now
a very fat man with a disagreeable habit
of snorting in cold weather. How gladly
the chaperon's thoughts fly away from
him, living, substantial, commonplace,
to the poor fellow who died at sea on
his way home from that horrid war in
Afghanistan.   How strangely

And Death.   true it is that were it not for
grisly Death, and pain and grief, there
would be no true romance in all the
world.   If every life were an epic, or
an idyll, would not both be commonplace?

LIGHTHEARTEDNESS.

OH ! what a delightful quality it is, both to the possessor and his friends. Lightheartedness is some-times confused with "animal spirits," but it is not at all the same thing. The latter we share with the young lambs in the meadows, the young goats on the rocky hillsides, the merry schoolboy in the days of his irresponsible youth, and the madcap schoolgirl who thinks those hours lost that are not spent in laughing. Light-heartedness is ingrained in the very nature of those who enjoy it ; while animal spirits are merely one of the exterior circumstances, incident to youth and health in a world that was created happy, and will never lose traces of that original Divine intention. Cheerfulness, again, is distinct from both. Men are always telling women that it is the duty of the less-burdened sex to meet their lords and masters with cheerful faces ; and if any doubt were felt as to the value of the acquirement— for cheerfulness often has to be acquired and cultivated like any other marketable accomplishment —shall we not find a mass of evidence

Light-heartedness and animal spirits.

Cheerfulness.

in the advertisement columns of the daily papers? Do not all the lady-housekeepers and companions describe themselves as "cheerful"? Lone, lorn women could scarcely be successes in either capacity, and cheerfulness is a distinct qualification for either post. A sort of feminine Mark Tapleyism must occasionally be needed to produce it, and keep it in full bloom.

Well, 'tis our duty to be cheerful, and those of us that are lighthearted have no difficulty about it. The *In trouble and work.* quality survives troubles of every sort, and lifts its possessor over many a Slough of Despond, into which the heavy-hearted would sink and be overwhelmed. And what a boon is lightheartedness when there is work to do! The man who whistles over his carpentering is happy, and his work is all the better for it. The mother who is chirpy in the nursery finds it an easy matter to manage the youngsters. They adore her bright face. And there are women who keep up this delightful sunniness of disposition well on to seventy years.

> " The world that knows itself too sad
> Is proud to keep some faces glad,"

says Owen Meredith, and it is good to see the happy twinkle in some aged eyes.

In married life there comes a time

when the romance of love, like a
glorious " rose of dawn," soft-
ening down into the steady
light of noonday, becomes
transmuted into a comfort-
able, serviceable, everyday friendship
and comradeship. In the same way the
animal spirits of youth often fade with
maturity into a seriousness which is
admirable in its way, a serenity which
keeps a dead level of commonplace.
If there is no natural lightheartedness to
fall back upon, there then arises the
everyday man or woman, with countenance composed to the varied businesses
of life, and never a gleam of fun or
humour to be found in eyes or lips.
They go to the play on purpose to
laugh, and enjoy themselves hugely in
the unwonted exercise of facial muscles ;
but for weeks between whiles they seem
unconscious of the infinite possibilities
of humorous enjoyment that lie about
them. It needs the joyous temperament
to extract amusement from these. If
that is absent the fields of fun lie fallow.
At a recent entertainment for children a
boy employed in selling chocolate
creams cried his wares in such
a lugubrious tone of voice
as to be highly inconsistent
with their inviting character.
"Chocklits ! " " Chocklits ! " he groaned
on the lower G, as though he had
been vending poison for immediate
use. Only two of the children present
saw the fun of this. And so it is with

With advancing years.

The humours of life.

these endless unrehearsed effects of daily life. The lighthearted seize them and make of them food for joy. And lightheartedness is of every age, from seven to seventy-seven and perhaps beyond it. Was there not once a blithe old lady who lived to the age of 110, and died of a fall from a cherry tree then ?

The joyous natures have their sorrows :—

"The heart that is earliest awake to the flowers
Is always the first to be touched by the thorns."

They have their hardships, their weary times, their trials of every sort, but the inexhaustible vivacity inherent in them acts as wings to bear them lightly over the bad places, where wayfarers of the ordinary sort must be broadly shod to pass without being engulfed. It is practically inextinguishable, and it makes existence comparatively easy.

"The merry
heart."

"The merry heart goes all the day,
The sad tires in a mile-a."

The chief enemy of lightheartedness is the constant companionship of the grim, the glum, the gloomy, and the grumpy, the solemn and the pragmatical. Who shall compute what bright natures suffer in an environment like this ? Day after day, to sit at table opposite a countenance made rigid with a practised frown, now deeply carved upon the furrowed

The enemy.

brow ; to long for sunshine and blue skies, and be for ever in the shadow of a heavy cloud ; to feel that every little blossom of joyfulness that grows by the wayside is nipped and shrivelled by the east wind of a gloomy nature ; this, if it last long enough, can subdue even lightheartedness itself ; can, like some malarial mist, blot out the very sun in the heavens from the ken of those within its influence.

More pains should be taken to develop the sense of fun and the possibilities of humorous perception of girls and boys. They should be taught to look at the amusing side of things. But teachers are so afraid of "letting themselves down," of losing dignity (especially those who have none to lose !), that they cannot condescend to the study of the humorous. Oh, the pity of it ! For it tends to the life-long impoverishment of their pupils.

The cultivation of humour:

A BIT OF EVERYDAY PHILOSOPHY.

THE French have a verb for which we
English have no equivalent. It is
"*savourer*," which in one
A useful verb. dictionary is translated "To
savour; taste with pleasure;
relish; enjoy." It sounds rather a
greedy word, and would indeed be so
if it applied only to the pleasures of
the table. But fortunately there are
for most of us other delights in life
than those connected with the gusta-
tory organs, and it is these that we
would fain *savourer*, as Linnæus did
when he fell on his knees on first
seeing gorse in bloom, and thanked
God. "How gross," remarks a character in a modern novel, "to give
thanks for beef and pudding, but none
for Carpaccio, Bellini, Titian!" Just
so. And apart from the deep appreciation of genius, have we not a
thousand daily joys for which we might
give thanks, if only we could attain to
the realisation of them? We let them
pass us by, and but vaguely recognise
them as bits of happiness which, if
duly woven into the woof of life,

would brighten it as no jewels ever could. It is good to encour-

The love of simple pleasures. age the love of simple pleasures. It is the way to keep our souls from shrinking. For some of us the song of the lark is as exquisite a pleasure as any to be found in the crowded concert-room. Both are delights, but the compass of the spirit may not always be great enough to embrace the two. To listen to the voice of a Patti is not possible to us all, even only once in a lifetime, and alas! there is but one Patti! Du Maurier says a lovely thing about her singing : " Her voice still stirs me to the depths, with vague remembrance of fresh girlish innocence turned into sound." With other singers the critical spirit of the audience is apt to awake and spoil everything. Music must be perfect, to be perfectly enjoyed. And how often do we find perfection in the concert-room? With how many singers can we let ourselves float far from reality into the region of the ideal,

On human and other songsters. secure from jar of false note, or twisted phrase to suit the singer? ·And have we not often to shut our eyes because the frame in which the golden voice is bodied is in dissonance with its beauty? With the lark we are safe, and the nightingale sings no false note. The robin is plump, but never fat and shiny! The plaintive cry of the plover is not spoiled for us

by a vision of some thirty teeth and
pink parterres of gum. Our enjoyment
of the blackbird's mellow whistle is
not marred by a little printed notice to
the effect that he craves the indulgence
of the audience as he has been attacked
by hoarseness ; and the flute-like
melody of the thrush has not its
romance eliminated by a stumpy figure
or want of taste in dress. Do I not
remember a great contralto singing to
us some stirring strains and wearing
the while an agony in yellow and grass-
green ? And did not even S—— himself alter the last mournful phrase of
" The Harp that once " into a wild top-
yell in order to suit his voice ? No !
With nature's choristers we are safe.

But do we half appreciate them ?
Not half, I am very sure. Do we give
thanks for the blue of the
skies, the green of the trees,
the sweet air that we breathe,
the glowing sunset, and the
starlit heavens ? It is true philosophy
to *savourer bien* these inexpensive joys ;
and, oddly enough, the more we do so
the less we shall feel inclined to
grumble and feel discontented when a
pall of dingy fog hides away the blue
and dims the green and gives us sulphur
to breathe instead of the lovely air
that invigorates and rejoices.

We owe an enormous debt to the
writers of books, and especially to
biographers of interesting lives, to
novelists, travellers who write of what

Our
ungrateful
folly.

they have seen and thus share their experiences with us, poets who sing down to us of the sunny heights of the ideal life, and those photographic story-tellers who delineate for us the workers of our world, of whose lives we should otherwise know so little. It almost rises to the height of epicurean philosophy to increase the joys of life by realising them to the full as they deserve to be realised. An hour spent with some delightful author may seem a little thing, but it is well worth saying grace for.

Things to be thankful for.

I forget who was the good man who, having been engaged to the girl of his heart for ten long years, made up his mind one day to ask her to allow him to kiss her, and who fervently said grace both before and after the operation. He was a philosopher! To possess a grateful spirit is to increase the happiness of life. Nature is so liberal with her good gifts that we take them too much as a matter of course. "How blessings brighten as they take their flight!" If sudden blindness were to fall upon us we should then find out too late how many pleasures come to us through the eyes.

Gratefulness indeed!

"Must our cedars fall around us ere we see the light behind?" It is good to teach young people to appreciate the infinite, everyday pleasures that

Appreciating everyday pleasures.

surround them. It adds immensely to their happiness, and their natural animal spirits will not be apt to disappear with youth as they too often do. There is a sort of cultivation for them in appreciation of the pleasures of art and science, apart from the mere knowledge they pick up. They can see the sunlight through the cedars and the moonlight through the waving branches of the pines. And what a feast life may be for the young in these days, when literature, art, and science are all brought within reach of the people. To hear one of Sir Robert Ball's lectures on astronomy is an introduction to a new world, a world that is immeasurable by any mere mortal thought. Pictures, sculpture, and the modern marvels of photography " come not in single spies, but in battalions." The heirs of all the ages are wealthy indeed. They can never count their riches, and usually neglect them because they cost nothing. Free libraries and public picture galleries all over the land are caviare to the general, though some find manna and nectar in them, and human working bees find honey.

Another secret of happiness in daily life is the appreciation of the friendship and affection which we

Another secret of happiness.

are inclined to hold but lightly until we are threatened with their loss. To awake to a full sense of its value is to learn to appreciate it as we never did before.

A BIT OF EVERYDAY PHILOSOPHY.

The young mother with her children about her is apt to let small worries cloud over the happiest time of her life. When she looks back at it, when the young ones have all grown up and gone from her, she wonders at herself for having ignored home joys. Children are troublesome, no doubt, and they are noisy little creatures and anxieties to boot. "A child in a house is a wellspring of pleasure," says Martin Farquhar Tupper, a writer already forgotten, but one who said many a true thing. A child in a house is also a wellspring of worry, many a mother might add, but would she be without it? Not for worlds. She is happier far than she knows. If she would only realise it she would be less likely to be sharp-tempered to the little troublesome darlings that crowd about her when she is busy, a sharpness that brings sometimes a sting of terrible remorse in its train.

> " If we knew the baby fingers,
>   Pressed against the window pane,
> Would be cold and stiff to-morrow—
>   Never trouble us again—
>
> Would the bright eyes of our darling
>   Catch the frown upon our brow ?—
> Would the prints of rosy fingers
>   Vex us then as they do now ? "

And with friends we have little estrangements that are not in the least worth while, if we would only realise it. Life is so short that there should

A BIT OF EVERYDAY PHILOSOPHY

be no room for squabbles! To walk
on the sunny side of the way
is wisdom, but how many of
us are wise? There are some
who diligently gather up the thorns
and fix their gaze upon the clouds.
Far better store the sunbeams and
enjoy the roses!

The sunny side.

"Strange we never prize the music
    Till the sweet-voiced bird has flown ;
Strange that we should slight the violets
    Till the lovely flowers are gone.

Strange that summer skies and sunshine
    Never seem one-half so fair,
As when winter's snowy pinions
    Shake their white down in the air!"

DEADLY DULNESS.

"We sit with our feet in a muddy pool, and every day of it we grow more fond."— RUSSIAN POET.

NINETY out of every hundred women bury their minds alive. They do not live, they merely exist. After girlhood, with its fun and laughter and light-heartedness, they settle down into a sort of mental apathy, and satisfy themselves, as best they can, with superficialities —dress, for instance. There are thousands of women who live for dress. Without it the world for them would be an empty, barren place. Dress fills their thoughts, is dearer to them than their children ; yes, even dearer than their pet dogs ! What could heaven itself offer to such a woman ? She would be miserable where there were no shops, no chiffons. The shining raiment of the spiritual world would not attract her, for she could not differentiate her own from that of others. And when beauty goes, and the prime of life with its capacity for enjoyment is long over, what re-

The apathetic majority.

9

mains to her? Nothing but deadly dulness, the miserable apathy that seizes on the mind neglected.

For it is pure neglect! To every one of us has been given what would suffice to us of spiritual life, but most of us bury it in the body, swathe it round with wrappings of sloth and indolence, and live the narrow life of the surface only. Scratching like hens, instead of digging and delving like real men and women, our true life becomes a shadow in a dream. Look at the stolid faces, the empty expression, the dull eyes, the heavy figures of all such! Do they not tell the tale of deadly dulness with its sickly narrative of murdered powers, buried talents, aspirations nipped in the bud, longings for better things suffocated under the weight of the earthly life?

Mental neglect.

We were never meant to narrow down to the circle of the home, in our thoughts at least. Yet this is what most of us do. To be domestic is right and good, but to be domestic only is a sinful waste of good material. Remember, oh massive matron! the days of girlish outlook into what seemed a rosy world. Think back to the days when it thrilled you to hear of high and noble deeds, when your cheeks flushed and your eyes brightened in reading of Sir Galahad and his quest, of the peerless Arthur and the olden days of chivalry,

Merely domestic.

when deeds of "derring-do" on battle-field or in the humble arena of life set the pulses throbbing with quick appreciation.

Is it all lost? Ali gone? Dead and buried? Is the spirit for ever outweighed by its fleshly envelope, The way out. the body? The earthly part of us is apt to grow overwhelming as the years roll on. But it can be fought against. We need not limit ourselves, as we so often do, to the daily round, the common task. There are wings somewhere about us, but if we never use them we shall soon forget we have them. What dwindled souls we have after a long life, some of us! "Whom the gods love die young," with all their splendid possibilities undamaged by the weight of the flesh. But we can avert the awful apathy of the spirit if we will. We can live full lives, if only sloth will let us. Indolence is the enemy who steals our best and brightest part, and opens the door to the dulness that settles down upon us, brooding over the middle-aged, and suffocating the mental life.

How many of us women read the newspapers, for instance? The great world and its doings go on Cultivating unheeded by us, in our wider sympathie absorption in matters infinitesimally small. We fish for minnows and neglect our coral reefs. "We deem the cackle of our burg the murmur of the world." It fills our ears

to the exclusion of what is beyond.
And yet the news of the universe, the
latest discoveries in science, the newest
tales of searchings among the stars, to
say nothing of the doings of our own
fellow creatures in the life of every day,
should be of interest. But we think
more of the party over the way, and
the wedding round the corner. Is it
not true, oh sisters ?

The more we stay at home, the less
desire we have to go out and about, to
freshen our thoughts, enlarge
A fatal error. the borders of our experiences, and widen our sympathies. It is
fatal. We sink deeper daily in the
slough of dire despond. But it should
be struggled against. There are lives
in which the duly recurrent meal-times
are absolutely the chief events. Think
of it ! Is such a life ignoble ? At
least, it contains no element of the
noble, the high, the exalted.

> " My sheathed emotions in me rust,
> And lie disused in endless dust."

So sings a poet of the day, and he
expresses for us what we must all feel
in moments of partial emancipation
from the corroding dulness that threatens
to make us all body, with no animating
spirit.

To associate freely with our fellow
creatures may not be a complete panacea
for this dreaded ill, but it at least will
take us out of our narrow selves to some
degree.

DEADLY DULNESS.

"A body's sel's the sairest weicht,"
when it is unillumined by a bright spirit.
And every spirit would be bright with
use if we but gave it a fair chance.

"Thou didst create me swift and bright,
   Of hearing exquisite, and sight.
 Look on Thy creature muffled, furled,
 That sees no glory in Thy world."

Perhaps we are too comfortable in our
apathy and ignorance, in our cosy homes
and pretty rooms, by our
bright fires, and surrounded
by the endless trivialities of
life, to look beyond. We are "pro-
vincial" in our thoughts, circumscribed,
cabined, cribbed, confined, for want of
being thrust forth to achieve our own
seed time and harvest, that inner garner-
ing with the real labour of which no
stranger intermeddleth, save to encourage from without, or the deeper to
enslave the mind in deadly dulness.

Pro-vincialism.

There are "comfortable couples" who
live together for half their lives, and in
mutual sympathy help to
deaden in each other every
wish for higher things. An
unhappy marriage is better
than this accord in common things, this
levelling down of the spirit to the
commonplaces of existence.

"Com-fortable couples."

Novel-reading is a considerable factor
in flattening and deadening the mind.
Fiction, to those who do not
misuse it, is the most delightful recreation, an escape from
the material to the airy realms of fantasy.

Novel-reading.

133

But there are girls and women who spend hours of every day in reading novels. "Three a week," one girl confessed to not long since. The mind soon gets clogged with overmuch fiction for food. It should never be allowed to supersede general reading. In this case it is idleness, nothing more, and tends to the encouragement of that mental indolence which soon enslaves the soul.

Women who have the command of money, and who might turn it to such noble uses in a world of suffering and sadness, spend enormous sums in playing games of chance or backing horses to win. When they lose, their irritability is a source of discomfort to all around them—and they generally lose ! Others play cards, risking high sums of money, and endeavour to create by this means, some interest in life. They little know what stores they have within them, lying ignored and neglected —almost forgotten. The more numerous our sources of pleasure the fuller and wider will be our lives. Even pain and suffering play their part in life, in living, and it is cowardice to shirk our full development for fear that it may entail some sorrow and deep-felt pang of sympathy that is helpless to assuage the sadness of a troubled world. Anything is better than deadly dulness, which rusts our faculties, benumbs our feeling, dulls our appreciativeness of all that is

Remedies worse than the disease.

The penalty of cowardice.

above and beyond us, and lowers us to the level of inanimate creation. Who would choose the existence of a cabbage when she might disperse her thoughts among the stars ? Who would be content with the comfortable hearthrug-life of a pet dog or tame cat when she might explore the recesses of science Possibilities. in company with masterminds, soar to heaven's gate in spirit, and expand in intelligence until she felt herself a part of infinity ? Contentment is ignominious, when it deprives us of our birthright. Let us, rather, be disconsolate till we attain it. Till then, Divine is Discontent.

THE PLEASURES OF MIDDLE AGE.

IN some lives middle age is far happier than youth, with its tumults, its restlessness, its perpetual effervescence, its endless emotions. Youth looked back upon from the vantage ground of middle age is as a railway journey compared with a summer day's boating on a broad, calm river. There was more excitement and enjoyment attached to the railway journey, but the serene and peaceful quiet of the pleasant drifting and the gentle rowing are by no means to be despised.

Youth and middle age.

When youth first departs a poignant regret is felt. So much that is delightful goes with it, especially for a woman. About thirty years of age, an unmarried woman feels that she has outlived her social *raison d'être*, and the feeling is a bitter one, bringing with it almost a sense of shame, even guilt. But ten years later, this, in its turn, has passed, and a fresh phase of experience is entered on. One has become hardened to the gradual waning of youth, and the

Crossing the half-way ground.

136

loss of whatever meed of attractiveness may have accompanied it. New interests spring up, especially for the married woman, with home and husband and children. The girls are marrying and settling down in their new homes, and the sons are taking to themselves wives, or establishing themselves in bachelor quarters, where they may live their own lives according to their own plan.

The loss of the young ones is acutely felt at first, but after a while the fresh voices and gay laughter are **The period of** less missed in the home, and **adjustment.** the sense of loneliness begins to pass away. The sons who called or wrote so frequently at first, missing the father's companionship and the mother's tenderness, begin to fall off a little in their attentions, and are sometimes not seen for weeks at a time. The daughters become more and more absorbed in their own home lives, and though they seldom fall off in duty to the father and mother as sons do, their heart is less and less in the matter. It is inevitable ! There is sadness in it, but no deep grief, as a rule. As the ties slacken, one by one, to be only now and then pulled taut, when occasion for sympathy in joy or sorrow arises, the process is so gradual and so natural that it is robbed of suffering. And as one of Nature's decrees is that which causes us to adjust ourselves to altered surroundings after change or loss, we accept the altered circumstances, and allow our thoughts

and feelings to grow round what is left
to us.

And then comes a strange and
beautiful aftermath, when there is a harvest of intellectual pleasures
The and the revival of a joy in
aftermath. life. Many and many a
project, formed in younger days, but
forgotten or submerged in the fulness
of existence during intermediate years,
is carried out during this late Indian
summer, when health and spirits, energy
and capacity, seemed to have renewed
themselves like the eagle. Music, long
neglected, begins again to play a happy
part in the lives of some. In others,
the brush is taken up after long years of
abstinence, and the alchemy of art
transforms into beautiful fruitfulness
what else might have been a barren
desert, now blossoming like a rose ; or,
journeys into far lands, longed
Compensa- for all through life, are at last
tions. undertaken, with an eagerness
of delighted anticipation that would not
disgrace youth itself. This wonderful
world is explored with keenest curiosity,
with results of strange and unexpected
enrichment of heart and brain. Is it not
true that the more we see of human
nature the more lovable we find it ?
Contrast the broad views and generous
charity of those who have travelled far
and wide with the censorious and
critical attitude of the women who
measure themselves by themselves and
compare themselves with themselves.

THE PLEASURES OF MIDDLE AGE.

A wider outlook and a broader grasp
of circumstances are among the consequences of living a fuller life.

There are, it is true, women who,
though they may stay at home through
all their lives, are incapable
Insular natures. of the carping criticism, the
inexhaustible reprobation,
and the endless hard judgments in
which so many of the members of
our sex indulge when youth is past
and they begin to be embittered. Even
these might be cured of lack of charity
by a more comprehensive knowledge of
the world and its inhabitants ; by freeing
themselves from insular prejudices and
a sort of provincialism of opinion that
is the outcome of narrow and limited
experience. Some of them, at least,
might benefit in this way ; but it is to
be feared that there are a few in whose
nature harshness is inherent, and whose
leisure will always be spent in deriding
the motes they so distinctly see in their
neighbours' eyes. They have scarcely
sufficient kindliness to try to get them
out.

There have been cases in which some
unsuspected talent has been developed
in middle age. It has lain
Dormant talents. dormant through all the
years when domestic life has
claimed the finest and best of a woman's
energies, and with leisure has come the
opportunity for displaying itself, and
making for something in the life of its
possessor. Women of middle age are

now being appointed to various posts of a semi-public character, such as inspectors of workrooms under the Factory Act, washhouses and laundries, and Poor Law guardians. In almost every case the appointments have proved satisfactory, conscientious care being bestowed upon the duties and a praiseworthy diligence being exhibited. But in some instances a peculiar and not too common gift of organisation has been evolved in discharging such offices, surprising the individual herself as much as those who are associated with her. No promise of it appeared in youth, but here it is in middle age, a quality that would for ever have remained unguessed and unutilised had life been accepted with folded hands as so many accept it, alternating between dining-room and drawing-room and daily drive, with no greater interest than the affairs of neighbours.

New occupations.

Youth is delightful, glorious, a splendid gift from the gods, but half realised while we have it, only fully appreciated when it is gone for ever. But let no young creature imagine that all is gone when youth is gone! Sunsets have charms as well as sunrise; and incomparable as is " the wild freshness of morning," there is often a beautiful light in the late afternoon. The storm and stress are past, and the levels are reached, after the long climb to the

After the storm and stress!

uplands. We still feel the bruises we sustained in the long ascent, but the activity of pain has passed, and we have learned the lesson of patience, and know by our own experience what youth can never be induced to believe —that Time heals everything. We can cull the harvest of a quiet

The joy of the harvest.

eye, and our hearts are at leisure from themselves. Cheerfulness, and even brightness, replace the wild spirits of girlhood, and our interests, once bound within the narrow channel of a girl's hopes and wishes, and then broadening only sufficiently to take in the area of home, are now dispersed in a far wider life. Philanthropy finds thousands of recruits among middle-aged women, and many of such beginners rise to the rank of generals and commander - in - chief. Youth is always looked back upon with a sentiment of longing, but

In praise of mellowing years.

middle age does not deserve to be decried. One, at least, who has attained it, can testify that at no other period of her life could she more intensely enjoy the lark's song, the freshness of the spring meadows, the beauty of the summer fields and woods, the pleasures of music and painting and oratory, and of new scenes and fresh experiences in a world that seems inexhaustibly novel the more we know of it. There are long, monotonous days in girlhood when one ardently wishes for something to happen to make a change ; but in middle age life is full of interests, and days seem far too short for all that we should like to pack into them. There is no monotony in middle age if health is good and the energies are kept alive by congenial work. Nor is the exultant joy in mere living quite dead within the heart of middle age. It breaks out now and then on a bright spring day when the sun is shining and the lark is singing, and when perennial hope points to yet brighter days to come. For hope sings songs even to the grey-haired, difficult as the young may find it to believe it. We were surely meant to be happy, we humans, so indomitable is the inclination towards joyfulness under circumstances the most adverse. It is easy enough in youth, and even the sceptic, the pessimist, the cynic, if they live long enough, will find that it is not so very difficult in middle age, when scepticism, pessimism, and cynicism are apt to be outgrown. There lies the true secret of the matter. There is a joy in growth, and we must see to it that we do not cheat ourselves of it. Stunted natures are seldom happy ones, and their middle age is merely mental shrinkage, with a narrowing of the heart and a corresponding drought in all the sources of joy.

"Hope springs immortal."

In one of Christina Rossetti's loveliest songs, she refers to the meeting in a better world of two who loved and were parted here. And in the last line she wistfully and pathetically asks : " *But shall we be young and together ?* " There lies the whole gist of the matter. If we are to be young again, what boots it if the loved faces of long ago are lacking? Could happiness be indeed happiness without these ?

The gist of the matter.

Sometimes two who have loved each other in their youth meet again when middle age has come to both. Such a meeting can never be commonplace to either. Nor do the two see each other as they are visible to ordinary acquaintances. In the eyes of memory, the grey hair is replaced by the sunny locks of youth ; the saddened eyes are bright again and eagerly out-looking into a world of abundant promise ; the worn and furrowed brow becomes smooth and white, the pale cheeks touched with youthful bloom ; and with a delicious sense of reciprocity each knows that the lost youth of both is present to the mind of either. Neither says inwardly of the other, " Oh, what a change ! " as is the case with ordinary acquaintances. Oh, no ! For each of these two the other is young again. They are both young again, and together. The gentle wraiths of past joys take them by the hand and lead them back to youth's enchanted land, to the days when love touched everything with a radiant

"After many years."

Memory's magic.

finger, turning the world and the future celestial rosy red.

What middle-aged women regret is the well-remembered friends that were their companions in the old days, "when morning souls did leap and run." And now they are "fed on minors" when they pause and listen to their thoughts and the rhythm that they make. "The world's book now reads drily," except, indeed, for such as are enwrapped and mummified in the garments of the reiterant daily commonplace.

"Fed on minors."

The only way to subdue regrets is to take the wider view, looking out on the great world as might a mouse from the granary door, over hill and dale and stream and distant town, blue sky and far green sea, realising how infinitesimally small a part of the whole is each individual life. There is a kind of comfort, after all, in insignificance. And can anything be more redolent of that quality than middle age?

The wider view.

"What is it all but a trouble of gnats
In the gleam of a million million of worlds?"

GROWING OLD.

To grow old is tragic, especially for women. Men feel it, too, there is small doubt. I once spoke on the *The common lot.* subject with one of the best-known men of up-to-date journalism, and we exchanged condolences on the passing of youth and the wild freshness of morning. We both agreed that at times we felt as bright and blithe, as merry and as full of fun, as in the days of our fleeting teens, though at times the world weighs heavily, and its burdens are duly felt.

We had each undergone an experience which, to thousands of others must be a landmark in the *In the eyes of the others.* years. It was not the first grey hair! That means nothing nowadays. Nor was it a touch of rheumatism. Do not babies of nine or ten experience that cramping ill? No! It was merely seeing ourselves as reflected from the mind of another. My companion had heard himself, in some legal proceedings, in which he had been a witness, described as a middle-aged man. With a shock of surprise he had realised that this really applied to him ! To every one of us comes this horrid moment of recognition. Feeling young, and with daily sight of ourselves unrealising the marks that Time indites upon our faces, we go on from year to year with a vague idea that we are always as we were, or nearly so. And then comes the rough quarter of an hour in which enlightenment arrives. It is good and salutary, but very unpleasant !

One of the most beautiful women I know, whose hair is prematurely white, with an exquisitely pic-

The inevitable moment. turesque effect of snowiness above the pink of soft cheeks, and the youthful light of deep grey eyes, was a little over forty when, talking one day with a comparatively new acquaintance, she was astonished to hear her say, " My husband says you are a dear old lady." " Old lady ! " The husband was, himself, her elder. The remark rankled for a long time, though I tried to convince her that only the most superficial and careless of observers would ever connect the idea of age with her.

The reason that women feel growing old so much more than men is that they know very well that they

Time, the thief. are more or less failures if they are not ornamental. Even the plainest of women can be decorative in her home surroundings so long as she has the bright eyes, fresh

146

cheeks, and the rounded, yet slight contours of youth. But after awhile Time begins "throwing white roses at us" instead of red, and every passing year puts into his laden wallet a little light from the eyes, a little bloom and softness from the cheeks, a little gloss and colour from the hair, a little lightness from the step, a little blitheness from the smile, and bestows upon us, in their stead, a varied assortment of odds and ends, which are, as to value, exactly what we choose to make them. It needs a little moral alchemy to turn them to gold and diamonds, pearls and opals ; and, failing this transforming touch, Time's exchanges seem sorry enough.

THREE WAYS OF GROWING OLD.

There are three ways of growing old. In two of them there lies a possibility of benefiting by the New Year's gifts of the old man with the scythe. The best way is to face things, and deliberately accept the situation, stepping out briskly to climb that steep bit of hill, and enter the shadows that lie beyond the crest. It is a good time to be optimistic. Like Mark Tapley's cheerfulness, it is most valuable in moments of depression. To believe, with Browning, that—

The best way.

"God's in His heaven ! All's well with the world,"

147

is the best restorative for sinking spirits that see the best and brightest part of life behind them, and shrink from the bleakness of old age that lies before them. To feel young in one's own thoughts and emotions is not always a consolation. The young ones have interests of their own, apart from ours. They may be too kind and gentle to let us perceive it, but there is almost always some *gêne* or constraint upon them in the presence of the middle-aged. They enjoy themselves more when in the society of their contemporaries. The expression of their faces, bright and sunny, tells us that. It clouds over with seriousness, if not with gloom, when they leave the young ones and share the companion-ship of the elders. The latter, if young at heart, feel this with many a recurrent pang ; but if they are elderly in their thoughts it gives them no trouble. They accept it calmly, as in the natural course of things. But with some of us it seems most unnatural that we should grow old. The whole being cries out against it, almost as urgently rebellious as we feel against an injustice. But all this emotion has to be conquered, and we have only to take ourselves in hand, once for all, and the thing is done. Let the young ones be happy in their own way. We had our day ! Let them have theirs. It will, at best, be sadly brief. Let them make the most of it.

Growing old in thought.

Regions to be conquered.

GROWING OLD.

THE SECOND WAY.

But there is a way of too freely submitting to grow old. A friend of mine sometimes says, " If you

Too easy submission. will insist on making yourself into a doormat you need not feel surprised if people wipe their boots on you." Quite so. Well, if we women lie down and regard friendly old Time as an inimical Juggernaut there is nothing to prevent us from sinking into dreary dowdiness, from wearing prunella shoes, and filling our husbands with the consternation that is inseparable from this elderly kind of footgear and false fronts. We need not too literally accept the warnings of disinterested friends, who think we should

Middle age and dress. be told that we " dress too young," or that the fashion of our coiffure is inappropriate to advancing years. Far better is it to dress too young than too old ; to keep our heads in consonance with the coiffures of the day than to date ourselves in any con-

Good sense. spicuous way. The women of our upper classes are sensible in this matter. So long as they can cover their heads with hair they do not wear caps. Not until seventy or so do they envelop themselves in the cumbrous mantles that once were devised especially for middle age, a period of life which, after all, is not adapted to weight-carrying. In travelling they wear hats or toques, and for everyday costume the tailor-made suit is generally adopted ; while for afternoon wear handsome and elaborate dresses are prepared. There is no reason why elderly women should carry weight for age when the latter becomes a disability instead of an advantage. And yet, in the fashion journals, as well as in the shops, all the heaviest and *A crushing* ugliest gowns, and all the *conspiracy.* least attractive of the mantles, to say nothing of the most hopelessly hideous bonnets, are presented to the elderly customer for her choice.

And with regard to other things, middle-aged women make themselves into doormats for Time to *Shining* tread upon. Because no en-*examples.* terprise or variety in life is expected of them, they never dream of originating any. There is no thought of foreign travel, of seeing all the interesting places where history is made, of keeping alive and awake and intent. It is only exceptional women, like the Duchess of Cleveland, Lord Rosebery's wonderful mother, who go round the world at seventy, and begin to write a book involving a visit to the eastern lands, where Lady Esther Stanhope, her great aunt, lived such a romantic life. Our Queen began to learn Hindustani when nearly seventy years of age. These shining examples are the ones to follow !

THE THIRD WAY.

The third way of growing old is to attempt to defy Time—regard him as an enemy to be thwarted, and endeavour to hide his detested ravages under a false array of cosmetics, dyes, and other appliances. It is a despicable and silly way, but one cannot refuse a meed of compassion to those who practise it. They are generally women who have been beautiful, and it is so hard to let beauty go without an attempt to detain her. It is a great gift, and to lose it is, to those who have possessed it, a terrible thing. Small wonder that they hug its remnants close, and wrap its rags about them. And, after all, the day must come when the tawdry imitations stand revealed for the useless things they are, even to those who pinned their faith upon them.

Defying time.

But time gives us all something in return ; a growing patience which brings sweetness and gentleness in its train ; a wider outlook on the world and a deeper insight into the hearts of friends ; a tender sympathy with those who suffer, and a truer sense of comradeship with our fellow-travellers on life's road. And all these things write themselves clearly enough on the ageing faces, sometimes beautifying what once was almost destitute of charm ; and some-

"The best is yet to be."

times spiritualising what once was beautiful in form and colour, but lacked the loveliness that results from an equal balance of mind and heart.

UNWIN BROTHERS, PRINTERS, WOKING AND LONDON.

MORE FACSIMILE REISSUES FROM PRYOR PUBLICATIONS

MANNERS FOR MEN

By 'Madge' of 'Truth'
Mrs Humphry

Seventieth Thousand

Like every other woman I have my ideal of manhood. The difficulty is to describe it. First of all, he must be a gentleman; but that means so much that it, in its turn, requires explanation . . .'

Marvellous Manners for Men.' — Time Out.

Originally published 1897.

Size 20cm x 10cm

76 Pages Paperback

ISBN 0 946014 23 X

£4.⁵⁰

MANNERS FOR WOMEN

By 'Madge' of 'Truth'
Mrs Humphry

Sixtieth Thousand

Can anything be nicer than a really nice girl'

'... *may seem quaint, but it is a useful reminde:*
that tittering is an unpleasant habit and curt
seying should be avoided unless you know wha
you are doing!' — The Time

"*Manners for Men* and *Manners for Women*
were written by Mrs Humphry and publishe
in 1897 ... I thought these reissues were bot
delightful and do hope they are hugely suc
cessful and help to bring back goo
manners." *Barbara Cartlan*

Originally published 1897.

Size 20cm x 10cm

164 Pages Paperback

ISBN 0 946014 17 5

£4.5

WHAT SHALL I SAY?

A guide to letter writing for ladies first published in 1898, this book, also written by Mrs Humphry, covers everything from a lover complaining of coldness to a lady who has experienced a sudden reverse of fortune. Also includes forms of address and 'Rules for letter-writing'.

Originally published 1898. Size 20cm x 10cm
132 Pages Paperback. ISBN 0 946014 25 6 **£3**.⁷⁵

Don't
A Manual of Mistakes & Improprieties more or less prevalent in Conduct and Speech

A best seller in the 1880s and once again in our facsimile edition (over 100,000 copies sold) *Don't* is a reflection of a society long since past. It makes for fascinating and amusing reading now.

Don't trouble people with your domestic mishaps, with accounts of your rebellious servants, or with complaints of any kind.

Don't neglect to keep to the right of the promenade, otherwise there may be collisions and much confusion.

Don't wear diamonds in the morning.

Originally published 1880. Size 13cm x 10cm
12 Pages. ISBN 0 946014 02 7 **£3**.⁷⁵

EVERYBODY'S BOOK OF CORRECT CONDUCT
Being The Etiquette Of Everyday Life

It is certain that he who lives correctly every day will find himself following the higher laws of morality and rectitude.' So says the Preface to this book that has contents ranging from The Duties of Life and The Pleasures of Life to The Formation of Habit; The Heart and Conscience, Conversation and Out-of-Door Life.

Originally published 1893. Size 13cm x 10.5cm
92 Pages Paperback. ISBN 0 946014 37 X **£4**.⁹⁹

THE NATURAL HISTORY OF STUCK-UP PEOPLE

ALBERT SMITH

'We are about to expose, as simply and truthfully as we can, the foolish conventionalities of a large proportion of the middle classes of the present day, who believe that position is attained by climbing up a staircase of moneybags.' Delightfully illustrated.

Originally published 1847. · *Size 13cm x 10.5cm*

128 Pages Paperback, Illustrated. ISBN 0 946014 39 6 **£3.99**

Albert Smith was one of the greatest showmen of the 19th century. His entertainments were as popular a feature of the capital as Madame Tussaud's and the Tower of London. This book was one of a series of fictionalised accounts that were very popular with Victorian readers.

EVERYBODY'S BOOK OF EPITAPHS

Being For The Most Part What The Living Think Of The Dead

Here lies my wife, a sad slattern and shrew
If I said I regretted her, I should lie too!

A look at epitaphs for the famous to the poor — some amusing, some sad, some historic, some enlightening, all fascinating.

Here lies John Wherdle, Parish Beedle
Who was so very knowing
His wisdom's gone, and so is he,
Because he left off growing.

Originally published 1885. Size 13.5cm x 10.5cm

128 Pages Paperback. ISBN 0 946014 38 8 **£4.50**

A PLAIN COOKERY BOOK FOR THE WORKING CLASSES

Charles Elme Francatelli, Late Maitre d'Hotel and chief cook to Her Gracious Majesty Queen Victoria

'My object in writing this little book is to show you how you may prepare and cook your daily food, so as to obtain from it the greatest amount of nourishment at the least possible expense, and thus, by skill and economy, add, at the same time, to your comfort and to your comparatively slender means.' Charles Elme Francatelli.

Contains over 240 recipes, including 'Baked Bullocks Hearts', 'Sheep Pluck', 'Cow Meal Broth' and 'Rice Gruel, a Remedy for Relaxed Bowels.' There are also sections on Cookery and Diet for the Sick Room and Economical and Substantial Soup for the Poor.

Originally published 1861. Size 14.9cm x 10.4cm

112 Pages Paperback. ISBN 0 946014 15 9 **£4.00**

A full list of our publications sent on request. All books post and packing free
PRYOR PUBLICATIONS
75 Dargate Road, Yorkletts, Whitstable, Kent CT5 3AE.
Tel/Fax: (01227) 274655